Books by Volker Heide

No More Tears: Sermons of Hope in Christ

God's Punch Line: Sermons of Life in Christ

The Key is Love: Sermons of Faith in Christ

Let Go and Let God: Sermons of Grace in Christ

Christ is the Center: Sermons of Mercy in Christ

Live By Faith! Sermons of Peace in Christ

Bless the Lord, O My Soul: Studies in the Psalms

The Lord is My Rock: More Studies in the Psalms

On Eagles' Wings: More Studies in the Psalms

At the King's Table: Studies in Luke's Gospel

Crash Course in Mormonism

*Available on Amazon
In Paperback and Kindle*

2

3

GOD'S PUNCH LINE

Volker Heide

King of Kings Publishing
Madison, Connecticut

4

Foreword

This book can give you a new beginning in your life. Discover a true and living hope. Find forgiveness in Jesus Christ, the Son of God. He is the compassionate Savior who loves you.

These sermons look at many favorite Bible Readings and you are encouraged to read the Bible passages listed for each sermon beforehand. Spend some time reflecting upon these readings.

The Word of God is powerful and effective. The Bible declares that God cares about you and promises to provide for all of your needs.

Let these sermons lead you deeper into the Word of God. Read the Bible everyday. Study the Scriptures. In the Bible, you can find the answers you are looking for. In Christ, there is always hope!

6

GOD'S PUNCH LINE

Featuring:

8

GOD'S PUNCH LINE: Luke 24:1-12

Today, we remember that Easter is a time for joy and laughter. After the seriousness of Lent and all the heaviness of Holy Week, Easter is a time to lighten up and smile. It is a time to enjoy God's punch line.

For example, Joseph of Arimathea was a wealthy Pharisee, a member of the Jewish ruling council and a secret follower of Jesus. It was Joseph who went to Pilate and asked for the body of Jesus after the crucifixion. He also supplied his own tomb for our Lord's burial.

Well, the story is told that someone pulled Joseph aside and said, "Joseph! That was such a beautiful, expensive, hand-carved tomb. Why on earth would you give it to someone else to be buried in?" Joseph just smiled, and said, "Why not? He only needed it for the weekend!"

Christ's resurrection is God's joke on the devil, and I bet the devil must have been surprised to find that the tomb was empty. The power of death could not hold the Son of God.

In our reading for today, Luke shows that the resurrection of Jesus was something that no one anticipated. The women didn't expect what they found. The men didn't believe what the women told them, and Peter himself was completely puzzled by what had happened. It was an astonishing turn of events.

Luke says that the women went to the tomb early on Sunday morning. They found the tomb open and they went inside. The angels greeted them with the question, "Why do you look for the living among the dead? He is not here. He has risen! Remember how he told you, 'The Son of Man must be delivered into the hands of sinful men, be crucified and on the third day be raised again.'"

The women were completely amazed at the message the angels delivered. In the same way, the apostles were clueless about what had really happened, and Peter was left wondering to himself what had occurred. Here, we see three different reactions.

In the Bible, three is an important number. Three establishes a pattern. It is the number of completeness. We confess our faith in the three persons of the Trinity - the Father, the Son, and the Holy Spirit.

Three wise men visited the baby Jesus after he was born. Jesus took three disciples with him up to the Mount of Transfiguration (and inside the Garden of Gethsemane). Peter denied Jesus three times. Three men were crucified on Good Friday. Christ rose from dead on the third day. We could go on.

In addition, have you ever noticed that in many jokes, the third person often provides the punch line? For example, three men die and they find themselves at the pearly gates of heaven. St. Peter tells them that they can enter heaven, if they can answer but one simple question.

Peter asks the first man, "What is Easter?" The man replies, "Oh, that's easy. It's that holiday in November when everybody gets together, eats turkey, and watches football."

Peter shakes his head and goes on to the second man. He asks him the very same question, "What is Easter?" The man replies, "Easter is that big holiday in December when we put up a nice tree, exchange presents, and celebrate the birth of Jesus."

Peter then goes up to the third man, and again asks, "What is Easter?" This man looks Peter squarely in the eye and says, "Easter is the holiday where we remember how Jesus was crucified. He died and was buried in a nearby tomb which was sealed off by a large stone."

Peter smiles with delight. But then, the man continued, "Every year the stone is moved aside so that Jesus can come out, and if he sees his shadow, there will be six more weeks of winter!"

Notice how it is the third person who provides the punch line here. Three is an important number. And looking back through the Gospel of Luke, we find three accounts of people being raised from the dead. Three resurrections, but the third one will deliver God's punch line.

In chapter seven, Luke gives us the account of Jesus raising the widow's son at the town of Nain. While traveling about in his ministry of teaching and healing, Jesus encounters a widow leading the funeral procession of her only son.

Luke says that Jesus had compassion on this widow. When he saw her weeping, his heart went out to her and he said, "Do not cry." Then, the Lord went up and touched the coffin and those who were carrying it stood still. (It was an open casket, so to speak, a funeral bier.)

Jesus then said, "Young man, I say to you, get up!" And the young man sat up and began to speak. The Lord helped him down from the coffin and gave him back to his mother.

In chapter eight, Jesus raised the daughter of Jairus, the synagogue ruler. Jairus had asked Jesus to come to his house to heal his daughter, but she died before the Lord could arrive. Someone came from the house of Jairus and said, "Your daughter is dead. Don't bother the teacher anymore."

However, upon hearing this, Jesus said to Jairus, "Do not be afraid; just believe, and she will be healed." Some people laughed at him, knowing that she was dead. However, Jesus went up to her room, and he took her by the hand and said, "Little girl, I say to you, get up!" At once, she got up, alive. Jesus then told them to give her something to eat.

And now, in chapter 24, our reading for today, we have the account of our Lord's resurrection. This, of course, is God's great punch line to the entire world.

The resurrection of Jesus is God's punch line, and it declares that everything has now completely changed. God's saving work is done. The great turning point of all history has occurred.

Do you remember what the angels told the women at the tomb? The angels said, "Why do you look for the living among the dead? He is not here; he has risen! Remember how he told you, 'The Son of Man must be crucified and on the third day be raised again.'"

Luke specifically says, "Then, the women remembered the words of Jesus." Then, it all clicked together. Then, they got the punch line. The words of Christ made sense. It was all true! His promises are sure! When the Lord says something in his Word, you can believe it with all of your heart and soul.

It was necessary for the Son of Man to be delivered over into death. He had to be crucified. He had to deal with our sin problem, and take all of our guilt upon himself. He had to give himself into such suffering and death, so that we might receive forgiveness.

Jesus had to die on that cross for us and then be buried in the tomb. However, on the third day, he was raised to life. That resurrection of Jesus changes everything.

Now, a new life begins for us. This is not our old life of weakness and failure. It is a new life of faith and hope, conviction and courage. That life begins in the waters of Holy Baptism.

Baptism bestows life and salvation. We are born again by water and the Word. The Holy Spirit gives life as he connects us to the cross and resurrection of Jesus. In Baptism, the resurrection power of the Son of God flows into your life. God the Father accepts you as his child, and he declares, "My Son has risen from the dead, and he has risen for you. Because he lives, you too shall live."

And on the last day, our physical bodies will be raised from the dead and transformed to be like our Lord's glorified body. On that day, we will fully enter the perfect and complete life we all yearn for.

Then, our baptism into Christ will reach its completion as we are raised from the dead and glorified. That resurrection we experience on the last day is God's final punch line to the entire universe.

Then, we will begin to enjoy God's new creation. We will begin to experience complete peace, joy and happiness. We will smile and rejoice because we will have reached our final goal.

We all know that this current life we experience today is not what God originally intended for humanity. This life is often so difficult and hard. We all struggle with unhappiness and disappointment. We are filled with depression, worry and anxiety.

Sometimes we feel just like the widow of Nain or Jairus. We experience the loss of our loved ones and friends. Death hurts us deeply. We weep our tears of sadness and grief. We are filled with pain and hurt.

But that is exactly why we need to remember the words and promises of Jesus. We need to remember that he says, "I am the resurrection and the life. Whoever believes in me has everlasting life."

"Come to me, all you who are weary and burdened, and I will give you rest. Take my yoke upon you and learn from me, for I am gentle and humble in heart. Come and you will find rest for your soul."

"Peace be with you. Why are you troubled and why do doubts arise in your minds? Look at my hands and feet. It is I myself! Touch me and see, a ghost does not have flesh and bones, as you see I have."

When the Risen Lord appeared to his followers after his resurrection, they finally got God's punch line. Before that, they were puzzled and confused. They were at a loss to make sense of what had occurred. They were totally clueless.

Often we are like that, too. We need to open our hearts to the Easter message, and then, everything will fall into place for us. Then we will understand God's purpose for our life and his entire creation. Our confusion and uncertainty will disappear.

Now, we look to Lord by faith, and we hear him say, "Don't be afraid; just believe. I say to you, get up! Enter the new life I have won for you through my suffering, death and resurrection."

Christ says, "Come now, rejoice and sing! Smile and laugh – everything is going to be all right in your life, because from here on, you and I are going to walk together. I am with you! I will never leave you or forsake you."

One final thought. Did you hear about the two Roman soldiers who were guarding the tomb of Jesus? The stone had been rolled away, and the tomb was revealed as empty. The one guard looked inside, and then he says to the other one, "Well, now there's only one thing that's certain – taxes."

In our world, taxes are a certainty (and that is no laughing matter). However, just as certain, for all who believe in Jesus Christ, death has lost its sting. Death has been defeated and vanquished forever. No more tears! Death does not have the last laugh.

The last laugh belongs to God. And today, the Lord God says, "Why are looking for the living among the dead? My Son is not here; he has risen. Remember how he told you that all this was necessary. Remember how he told you."

That is the key - remember all the words Christ has spoken to you. Believe his promises with all your heart and soul. Believe and then you will experience the joy of a new life and the promise of the new creation to come.

Go ahead, smile. Rejoice and sing. The victory is yours! Christ has risen; he has risen, indeed. This is God's punch line delivered to you today. Amen!

LIVING AMONG THE WEEDS: Matthew 13:24-43 & Romans 8:18-27

There once was a farmer who owned the best land you have ever seen. One spring, he plowed, furrowed, and sowed in a big crop of wheat. Then, he sat back to let nature take its course.

First, there came the refreshing spring rains soaking the land. Then, the warm, summer sun drew the new plants to the surface of the soil. Soon, the whole earth was green with lush growth.

But then, something happened. One day, one of the field hands came and told the farmer, "Something's gone terribly wrong. Something else was sown in with the wheat. You've got some kind of weed in there, spoiling the whole crop. It must have been some bad seed that got mixed in at the beginning. We had better get in there, and start pulling up all those weeds."

But the farmer replied, "No, don't do that. If you pull up all the weeds, you might pull out some of the wheat, too. The wheat will be okay, and I don't want to lose any of it. Let it go. We can separate it all at the end, at the final harvest."

Now, what is remarkable here is that most farmers would probably just plow under a bad crop and completely start over. That would certainly be a whole lot easier than trying to separate all the plants at harvest time.

However, this farmer is different. His concern is that none of the good harvest be lost. "Let both grow together all the way to the end." And this is where we start to understand our story for today.

The way Jesus tells our parable leads us back to Genesis and the story of the fall. Our Lord says, "The kingdom of heaven may be compared to a man who sowed good seed in his field."

In the beginning, God created Adam and Eve to live in the Garden of Eden. They had a perfect life filled with happiness and joy. They had a lush, green paradise to live in and everything they needed. "God saw all that he had made and it was very good."

But then, an enemy came and sowed weeds among the wheat. The devil tempted Adam and Eve to sin and to rebel against God. That is when paradise and perfection were lost. That's when sin and death entered into this world. "When the plants came up and bore grain, then, the weeds also appeared."

In other words, the bad seed spoiled the field. The weeds appeared all over the place. The good crop was lost. God's good and perfect creation was spoiled by an enemy, the devil.

So, what does God do? Does he plow creation under and completely start over? Does he wipe out this universe and create another one? No, he lets the weeds and wheat grow together until the final harvest. "Let both grow together until the end."

And so, ever since the fall, we have been living among the weeds. That is the reality of life in this world today – we live among the weeds. We have good seed and bad seed all mixed together, and sometimes it's hard to figure out what is what. Our world is filled with evil, and we see it all around us every day.

This can be very confusing. And so, we all have our questions. "Master, did you not sow good seed in your field? Why does it now have so many weeds?"

We ask, "Lord, why is there so much evil and suffering in the world today? Why do so many bad things happen in my life?"

The answer to all these questions is that something happened to God's original work. An enemy came in and ruined the crop, and all of creation has been affected by this.

The fall has affected the entire universe, and that includes nature and humanity. We see that in what Paul says in Romans 8.

Notice, first of all, how Paul speaks of this present time and what is to come. Paul says, "I consider that the sufferings of this present time are not worth comparing with the glory that will be revealed to us. For all of creation waits with eager longing for what is yet to come."

Creation is waiting for something. That something is the last day when all things will be made new. Meanwhile, we live in a world filled with weeds. Creation is now subjected to frustration. It is in bondage to decay. It is groaning with the pains of childbirth. In other words, this present world is falling apart.

You can see that in the increasing natural disasters we are experiencing. You see more and more earthquakes, tsunamis, hurricanes, typhoons, volcanoes, flooding, drought, wildfires and other natural catastrophes.

You see it also in our society with increasing violence, crime, and bloodshed. Terrorism can strike us anywhere, at any time. Many parts of the world are on the brink of war. Hatred, discord and division are steadily increasing.

We also see this in our personal life with increasing family problems. We see troubled marriages, alcohol and drug abuse, broken relationships, and so many other things that bring us unhappiness and grief.

Life is becoming increasingly difficult to figure out. It seems like the weeds are taking over. However, we need to be careful here. There is another factor to consider, and this complicates things even more. We need to stop and realize that we are part of the problem. The truth is we are weeds, too.

We are weeds because we are sinners. We have spoiled our life and have made a mess of things. This problem of evil has infected our hearts, too. We are weeds, and it's a sorry state we find ourselves in.

But remember, Paul not only speaks of the sufferings of this present age, but he also speaks of the glory that is to come. Paul speaks of hope - the hope of a new creation, the hope of a new and better life.

This hope is possible because God himself has dwelt with our problem of evil. God has a solution to our fatal dilemma, and that solution is his Son.

Christ comes to save and restore a lost creation. He comes to undo the damage caused by the evil one. He comes to defeat our enemy, and he beats the devil at his own game.

The Son of God takes upon himself our flesh and blood. He humbles himself and becomes our servant. He experiences our life and enters our struggle.

And here we see how God himself enters his fallen creation through his Son. God himself becomes the seed that is sown in the field of this world.

And Christ grows up to become the One who will carry our burden. He takes all of our sin and guilt upon himself. He carries all of the evil of this world down into the very depths of hell. He becomes a weed as he suffers on the cross.

Our Lord is that weed that is thrown into the fires of hell. He suffers and dies for sins of this entire world. He is thrown into the fiery furnace of hell. He experiences our judgment and the punishment we deserve.

That is why God now declares that for the sake of Christ, "Your sins are forgiven!" For the sake of the innocent suffering and bitter death of God's only Son, you are declared righteous and holy. You are now a part of God's kingdom. You are God's beloved child. You are wheat!

Now, you have the hope of that new creation to come. By God's grace, you are wheat, and you are growing stronger each day, soaking up the waters of God's mercy, basking in the warm sunshine of God's love.

Our Lord transforms us from bad seed to good. He changes us from weeds into wheat. He transforms us from sinners into saints. That is Christ's saving work, and he does a good job at it. He brings salvation to a lost creation.

This is a salvation we have right now, by faith. We have not yet fully entered into it, but we hold onto the promise of what is to come. We hope for what we do not yet see. Moreover, we wait for this new creation with patience and perseverance.

At the present time, creation groans, and we groan as well. We still live in a world filled with evil, sickness, problems and heartache. Sometimes we sometimes feel absolutely overwhelmed by this rising tide of evil.

However, Paul says the Holy Spirit helps us in our weakness. The Spirit himself intercedes for us before God. Think about that! The power of the Holy Spirit is with you!

And the Holy Spirit is there each day for us. He helps us cope with the sadness and grief we experience. He helps us in times of confusion and uncertainty. He is there as we deal with family problems and the brokenness of daily life.

This present life certainly is filled with many unanswerable questions, and sometimes we do not know what to do about our problems. But the Spirit helps us in our weakness. He intercedes for us. He continually leads us back to our Savior, and back to the throne of the Father in heaven.

Therefore, who shall separate us from the love of Christ? Can trouble or hardship or suffering ever separate us from God's love? Can death, or even the devil himself, ever separate us from the love of God revealed through the cross and resurrection of his Son?

No, not even our worst enemy can ever separate us from God's love. He has been defeated by Christ. The devil is beat. The game is over, and you are victorious in Jesus.

The key is to always remember that you have this victory now, by faith. By faith, you look can forward to a better day and a new creation, a new world where there will be no more tears. This hope lifts up your eyes to see the glory that will be revealed on the last day.

It is true that we still live among the weeds. We still cope with suffering and endless tragedy. We still experience pain and hurt, and we still see terrible disasters all around the world.

But lift up your heart and look forward to the final harvest when God will make all things new. On that day, evil will be banished forever.

Look forward to that day of glory when all of creation will rejoice in the newness that God will create. Look forward with hope in Christ.

Let the Holy Spirit fill you with confidence. God is in control, and God knows what he is doing. He does not want any of his wheat to be lost. God wants all people to be saved and to turn to Christ, our Savior.

That is why the Father continues to reach out to the lost today. God says, "Receive the gift my Son has won for you! Receive this free gift of life and forgiveness. My grace can transform you into good seed. Receive the Holy Spirit who will produce a rich harvest in your heart, an abundance of wheat flowing over into life everlasting." Amen!

BECOMING RELIGIOUS: Luke 8:26-39

Today, Jesus sails across the Sea of Galilee to the opposite side, to the region of the Gerasenes. When the Lord got out of the boat, he encountered a strange man who was possessed by demons. He was wild and uncontrollable. He was violent and dangerous. In fact, he was kept under guard and was bound with chains and shackles. The guy was self-destructive.

The people nearby tried to help him, but the man would break all of these bonds and escape. The demons would then drive him deep into the wilderness. There, he lived among the tombs. This was a wild chaotic life, filled with pain and hurt and isolation.

And so, when Jesus got out of the boat he encounters this wild man. When the demon-possessed man saw Jesus, he cried out with a loud voice and fell down to the ground. He cries out, "What do you want with me, Jesus? I know you are the Son of the Most High God! I beg you, do not torment me!"

Jesus then asked him, "What is your name?" "Legion," the man replied (because many demons had entered him). Moreover, these demons were begging the Lord not to send them into the abyss.

Nearby, there was a large herd of pigs feeding on a hillside. The demons begged Jesus to let them enter the pigs. He gave them permission. The demons then entered into the pigs, and the herd goes crazy. The swine rush down a steep bank into the waters of the Sea of Galilee and they drown.

When the people heard about what had happened, they came out to see for themselves. They discover the man who was so violent and self-destructive calmly sitting at the feet of Jesus. He is once again in his right mind. He has been healed by Christ and set free from the demons that possessed him. He is quiet and calm, at peace with the world around him.

The people see all this and they are shocked. They become extremely alarmed and afraid. They promptly ask Jesus to leave. "Go away from us!" they say. "Get out of here!"

As the Lord is getting into the boat to depart, the man who has been healed wants to go along with him. However, Christ sends him back to his city. "Return to your home and declare to everyone how much God has done for you." And so, the man went away, proclaiming throughout the whole city how much Jesus had done for him.

Notice how the healed man equates the work of Christ with the work of God. He recognized that in Jesus of Nazareth, God has come to rescue us. God himself has come to heal and set us free. God comes to save and make all things new. Jesus Christ, the Son of God, comes to give us a new and better life.

Now, before this man was healed, he thought the exact opposite. When he first encountered Christ, he cried out, "What do you want with me? I beg you, do not torment me!"

Did you catch that? This man actually thinks that Christ has come to torment him. "O Lord, don't hurt me! Don't make my life so hard! Don't make me miserable and unhappy!"

Many people have this same attitude today. They have many weird and strange misconceptions about Christianity. They think Christ has come into this world to torment us, hurt us, and make us unhappy.

That is why many people reject Christ. They have their strange excuses. For example, some will say, "I don't believe in organized religion." In fact, I hear that quite often. People will say to me, "I don't want to become a Christian because I don't believe in organized religion." (And to that, I reply, "Well, I think you would like our church. We are pretty disorganized.")

Others will say, "I don't want to become religious right now. I want to have some fun first. Let me be happy. I'll join the church later, when I'm old."

This is the attitude that says, "Do not torment me with all this Christianity stuff. I want to be happy and live the good life first."

That is surprising, right? Some people really think God exists to make us unhappy. God wants to torment us and take away our fun and ruin our life. But really, the opposite is true.

We are the ones who torment ourselves. We are the ones who make ourselves unhappy. We mess up and ruin our own life. And we bring all kinds of chaotic demons into our life.

The truth is I often make my life way harder than it has to be. I try to do too much, and then I feel overwhelmed and stressed out. That's when life becomes torn and frayed.

Another problem is that many of us live in constant fear. We worry so much about our life, and we drive ourselves crazy by worrying about things that will never happen. Anxiety and restlessness plague our hearts. We feel trapped by fear.

Another problem is guilt and regret. We are hounded by a sense that our life is not what it should be. We struggle with remorse and guilt over the past. And we feel powerless to change this.

The demons we have to wrestle with are legion. In many ways, we are just like that man who lived among the tombs. We are wounded and hurt, trapped in our self-destructive behavior. We are running away from God and then wonder why our life is such a chaotic mess.

We need to discover once again that God comes not to torment us, but to save us. God comes to rescue us, to heal us and to set us free from the demons that would ruin our life. Look again and see how Christ helped this poor guy.

The Lord gives his command and the man is set free. Jesus speaks his Word and the demons are cast out. Just like that!

Before the man encountered Jesus, his life was a total wreck. Afterward, he sits quietly at the feet of the Lord, all calm and peaceful. Now, he is in his right mind. Life is what it should be. He has become religious in the best sense of the word.

The man now desires to be with Jesus continually. In fact, he even wants to get into the boat and sail off with him back to Galilee. This man wants to follow the Lord every day and live in his presence. He wants to listen to that powerful Word of God continually.

That is how it is when you encounter the Savior. He has the power to heal your wounds. He can set you free from your pain and hurt. His love can truly change you.

Remember, the Lord comes not to torment, but to bless. And Jesus says to you today, "Your sins are forgiven, go now in peace! Your faith has made you well. Return to your home and declare how much God has done for you."

That is what true religion is all about. Religion is about the God who loves you, the God who sends his Son to die on the cross for your sins. Jesus suffered and died for you, and then, he rose from the dead to give you a brand new life.

That word, "religion," is a Latin word. It comes from a root that means, "To bind together." Therefore, when a person becomes religious, they are being bound together by God. They are pulling their life together by the power and grace of God. Order and stability are being restored. Peace and calmness are filling their hearts and minds.

Ultimately, we cannot pull our life together by our own power and strength. We are just like the man possessed by the demons. He was absolutely trapped and in total bondage. There was no escape for him. But then, he met Christ.

The Lord Jesus is able to rescue you, no matter what demons you may be wrestling with today. He can set you free and bind up your life. He can heal your wounds and make you whole. He can bestow upon you that peace that passes all understanding.

This reminds me of the story of a man who was driving along the highway. He hits a big bump and hears a clang, but he ignores it and keeps on driving. When he got home, he discovered that one of his hubcaps was missing.

Therefore, the next day he goes back to the spot where he hit the big bump, and sure enough, there was his hubcap propped up on the side of the road. When the man walked over to get it, he noticed a note attached to the hubcap. It read, "Hi there! I've been waiting for you to find me!"

That is how it is for us. We were lying on the side of the road, all alone. We were lost, but now we are found. The Lord Jesus has come back to claim us as his very own. And the Savior finds us and binds up our broken life. He makes us whole again. He heals us with his powerful love and infinite forgiveness.

Therefore, rejoice and be glad! Give thanks for the Lord Jesus! Receive his gift and live in his grace. Listen to his Word continually and follow him every day in faith. Become religious (in the best sense of the word). Become religious and trust in Christ as your Lord and Savior.

And go and declare how much God has done for you in Christ. Go and tell others that there is hope. There is healing. There is the sweet freedom that Christ gives - the freedom of knowing you are loved by God and you belong to him forevermore. Go and tell everyone - there is a new and better life in Jesus. Amen!

A COLLISION WITH CHRIST: Matthew 16:21-28

Did you hear the story about the elderly lady who was driving a big, new expensive car? She was preparing to back into a parallel parking space. Just as she was about to back in, a young man in a small sports car zoomed into her space, beating her out of it.

The woman got out of her car and angrily demanded to know why he had taken her parking spot, when he could clearly see she was trying to park there. The man laughed and replied, "Because I'm young and quick!" And with that, he walked away.

A few minutes later, he comes back and finds the lady using her big, new car as a battering ram. She was backing her car up, and then ramming it into his parked car, over and over again. The collisions were tremendous!

The man cried out, "Why are you wrecking my car?" Her response was simple: "Because I'm old and rich!"

Our reading today describes a series of tremendous collisions. The first involves Peter. After the dust settles from that, we have another series of collisions.

Now, what's this all about? What causes such a commotion? Well, the situation is this: Peter has just confessed that Jesus is the Christ, the Son of the living God. Jesus is the Messiah, the promised Savior, the very of Son of God in human flesh.

Matthew then says, "From that time on, Jesus began to show his disciples that he must go to Jerusalem and suffer many things. He must be rejected and betrayed. He must be killed, and on the third day, be raised from the dead."

Note the great urgency in the words of our Lord. He must go to Jerusalem. He must be rejected, betrayed and killed. He must go to the cross to die for the sins of the world.

The Lord says that going the way of the cross is absolutely necessary. It must be so. There is no way to get around it. This is God's will. It is the Father's purpose and plan.

The same holds true for each of us. We also must take up our cross and follow Jesus. We must be willing to lose our life for the sake of Christ. We suffer with our Lord. We go the way of the cross.

Yet, going the way of the cross is the very last thing we would ever choose. Such cross bearing does not come naturally to us. This totally goes against our normal, natural way of thinking. We do not like hearing this. It makes us feel uncomfortable.

That is why when Peter hears these words of Jesus, he swiftly takes him aside and begins to rebuke him. "May this never happen to you, Jesus! God forbid that such a terrible thing would ever occur to you. Don't even talk like that!"

Here comes the first collision: The Lord Jesus immediately rebukes Peter and says, "Get behind me, Satan! You are a stumbling block and a hindrance to me. You are not setting your mind on the things of God, but on the things of man."

Can you hear the fierce determination in the voice of Jesus? Nothing will turn him away from going that way of the cross. Nothing will tempt him to disobey God's will. Nothing will cause him to avoid the terrible suffering that awaits him in Jerusalem.

Not the temptations of the devil, and not this suggestion of Peter, which is just like it. Peter just doesn't understand the things of God. He doesn't have a clue. He fails to comprehend God's purpose and plan for the Messiah. That is why Peter actually tries to talk Jesus out of going the way of the cross.

However, God operates in a way that is far different from ours. God's way is not our way.

His thinking is not like ours. His purpose and plan for our lives are not what we expect. That is why we have such tremendous collisions with God's will for us.

Watch now how Jesus takes everything one step further. He says, "If anyone would come after me, let him deny himself and take up his cross and follow me. Whoever saves his life will lose it, but whoever loses his life for my sake, will find it. What will it profit you, if you gain the whole world and yet forfeit your soul?"

Here, Jesus is saying to us, "If you really want to follow me and become my disciple, you have to take up your cross and walk in my footsteps. You must be willing to follow me to Jerusalem. You must suffer and die with me."

This means we embrace the cross of Jesus and make it our own. We totally give our life to the Lord, and we hold nothing back. This is a total surrender. We lose our old life in Christ as we follow him in faith. We die with him.

Here we encounter another collision with Christ. If it were up to us, we would totally avoid the cross. We would prefer to hang on to our current life. We hesitate to make a total commitment to our Lord. We would rather think that we are the ruler of our life and we have full autonomy.

Like Peter, we really don't like hearing all this talk about suffering and death. We don't want to go the way of the cross. But that is not the way of God's Messiah. He must go to Jerusalem and suffer many things. He must be killed, and then, be raised from the dead. All of this is absolutely necessary. It must be so.

That is exactly why Jesus says, "Follow me!" He says, "Put aside your natural way of thinking about your life and just follow me. Let go of your old life and follow me! Watch now what happens." And so, by God's mercy and grace, we simply follow Jesus in faith, and we see something amazing.

By faith, we follow him to Jerusalem. We follow him to the upper room where he celebrates the Last Supper. Then, we journey with him to the Garden of Gethsemane. We see how he is betrayed by Judas, arrested and taken away.

We follow him then as he stands before the Sanhedrin and is falsely accused. We watch as he stands before Pontus Pilate and is unjustly condemned. We see how the soldiers beat and flog him and spit upon him.

Then, we follow Jesus as he carries the cross to Golgotha. We are there as he is nailed to the wood. We see how he suffers and dies, and how he sheds his holy and precious blood.

Now, we continue to follow him into the tomb, and we enter with him inside. We are buried with him into death. The tomb is sealed tight.

In this way, by faith, we truly experience his suffering and death. We experience his burial and rest in the tomb. Then, we experience his glorious resurrection. You see, when you follow Jesus, you follow him all the way.

You follow him to the cross and you die with him. You follow him into his tomb. You buried with him into death. Then, by the power of God, you are raised up with Christ in his resurrection. Now, continue to follow Jesus by faith. Follow him all the way into heaven through his ascension. Now, his life becomes your life, and your life becomes his. You have lost your life in Jesus.

Again, when you follow Christ, you follow him totally, absolutely and completely. And when you give yourself totally to the Lord in this way, you finally discover the true life that only he can give. We find what we are looking for.

We lose our life in Jesus and find the true life God intended for us to experience from the very beginning. Jesus says, "If you want to live only for yourself, you're going lose out. But if you follow me, you can find true life."

Jesus says, "What good is it if you can gain the whole world, but end up forfeiting your soul? But whoever lives for me will find true life. Whoever follows me will find real joy and true peace and a lasting happiness."

One last point before we end. When you give your life to Christ, you can also give him everything else. You can give him all of your burdens. You can give him all of your fears and worries, all of your problems and heartaches. You can share with him all of your sadness and grief. You can give to him whatever burden you are carrying today.

The Lord shares our life and he also shares our burdens as well. That is the amazing thing about our Savior. He not only says, "Follow me," but he actually walks right beside us, each step of the way. He is there walking with you right now, empowering you to take up the cross.

The Lord Jesus helps us to bear the cross. He helps us to deal with suffering and pain. He gives us courage, strength, and the ability to keep on going, no matter what we may face.

Moreover, with our Lord's help, we can stop colliding with God's will for our life. We can accept God's ways. We can follow God's purpose and plan for us. No more collisions, just acceptance.

By God's grace, you can start setting your mind on the things of God. You can embrace the cross and make it your own. You lose your life in Jesus and find it each day.

And so, now we follow our Lord together, and we discover the true joy and confidence only he can give. We follow Jesus and we find something special and enduring. We discover that God's ways are always the best. We just need to trust in God's purpose and plan for us. Therefore, let us follow Jesus, and follow him all the way, until we enter that new creation that awaits us. Amen!

WE KNOW! Romans 8:28-39

Today, St. Paul says, "We know that for those who love God, all things work together for good, for those who are called according to his purpose."

Our text for today deals with a great problem in the lives of many people. The problem is that feeling that life has no purpose or meaning. Nothing really matters. We are at the mercy of fate or chance. Things just happen by accident.

Such a viewpoint can sour your outlook on life. But that is how many people think. We are victims of bad luck and ill-fortune. Life is random. Accidents happen. We are all trapped by fate and chance.

Now, as believers in Christ, we would reject that idea that life has no meaning or purpose. We do not believe that we are helplessly trapped by bad luck. We are not victims of fate and chance.

However, the trouble here is that we do not live theoretically; we live in the concrete realities of everyday life. Each day, we are confronted with situations that test our basic beliefs. Many unexpected things happen to us. Our faith is constantly put to the test.

And let's be honest – at times, such testing can lead to doubts. And doubt can lead to a lack of confidence in God. And if we think God is against us, we feel empty and hollow inside. We feel lonely, forgotten and afraid.

Without a doubt, we all have to put up with difficulties, heartaches, and endless problems. So many irritations can upset us. The people we encounter every day can provoke us and make us angry and upset.

Usually, such minor things can be handled easily enough, but when they are coupled with bigger problems, they seem to be part of a deeper pattern.

Our car breaks down just when we need it the most. We get sick at the worst possible time. Our kids have problems we have worked so hard to avoid. Our money runs out too soon. We are passed over for that promotion at work. Our loved one unexpectedly gets sick and dies.

We may joke about Murphy's Law – if anything can go wrong, it will, and at the worst possible moment – but in our private moments, we wonder. All these problems seem to part of a bigger pattern. As we search for explanations, we can go in several different directions.

We may consider that these things are a punishment sent to us from an angry God. We think, "God is out to get me! God is punishing me for something I have done." We say, "Why me, Lord? What do you have against me? What have I done to deserve this?"

Sometimes, we may mean that as a joke, but it's no joke when those questions are asked from an emergency room, or when we are sitting in the doctor's office awaiting some test results, or when we hang up the phone late at night after hearing some bad news.

Another direction we might go would be to think that God does not really care about us. We think God has forgotten all about us. Somehow, our life has just slipped through the cracks. We have dropped off into the void. Things just happen by chance or accident.

These are not new thoughts. Such thinking is common to all people, everywhere. We all struggle with such questions. What is the answer to our questions?

Listen again to what Paul says, "We know that for those who love God, all things work together for good, for those who are called according to his purpose."

Paul says, "We know!" And this is not the same as saying, "We think," or "We guess," or "This is our most plausible theory."

No, Paul says, "We know!" We know that this is absolutely true and certain. This is the real deal. This is the absolute truth. We know that for those who love God, all things ultimately work together for our eternal good.

We know that God is always faithful to his promises. We know that even in our present situation, whatever that might be, God has our best interests in mind. God cares.

I mean, think of a situation in your life right now where you are struggling. Think of a difficulty, problem, or heartache you are currently wrestling with.

Now apply this verse to that problem. Say to yourself, "I know that even in this great difficulty I'm going through right now, God is in control. All things work together for good, for those who are called according to God's purpose. God is at work in this situation!"

Here we are confessing that as far as God is concerned, there are no accidents or random occurrences. God is always in control. And God can work through anything to bring good into our life.

We know this is absolutely true because Paul also says, "If God is for us, who can be against us? He who did not spare his own Son, but gave him up for us all, how will he not also, along with him, graciously give us all things."

God has demonstrated his love for us beyond any doubt. He has sent his one and only Son into this world so that we might live through him.

"This is love, not we loved God, but that he loved us and has sent his Son to be an atoning sacrifice for our sins."

This is love – the Father gave his Son to pay the price for our sins. This is how much God loves you - this is how much he cares. He gave his one and only Son to suffer and die for you. Think about that!

This great and wondrous love of God now touches our hearts and it creates a response within us. When we discover that God loves us in such an amazing way, we begin to love God in return.

We now love God, and we know for sure that God is working in all things for our good. We are not forgotten or cast aside. God is for us!

Furthermore, we know that if the Father did not spare his own Son but gave him up for us all, he will also graciously give us all we need. God will give us the power and ability to cope with any problem we may face in this life.

Listen, God is for us; he is not against us. God is in control. We are not victims of fate or chance or Murphy's Law. The Lord God is in absolute control of everything that happens.

48

And God is not punishing us for our sins. If you want to talk about God punishing sinners, then let's go to the cross and see how Jesus was crucified. He took our place and became our substitute. He was punished for the sins of the whole world, and that includes us.

Let's not forget that the way God punishes sins is with eternal damnation in hell. That is exactly what Christ endured on the cross for us.

"While we were still sinners, Christ died for us." "God made him who had no sin, to become sin for us." "My God, my God, why have you forsaken me?"

On the cross, Jesus took our place and became our substitute. He made that perfect and final atoning sacrifice as he endured that punishment we all deserve. He was forsaken by the Father as he experienced hell and damnation on our behalf.

You have been redeemed by the blood of Christ. Your sins, all of them – past, present and future – are totally and absolutely forgiven. You have been redeemed by the blood of the Lamb. You have an absolute forgiveness.

This forgiveness bestowed by God for the sake of Christ has a great meaning and purpose. You were redeemed for a specific reason.

Paul tells the Ephesians, "For we are God's workmanship, created in Christ Jesus to do good works, which God has prepared in advance for us to do."

This is what it means to be redeemed according to God's purpose. The Lord has a definite plan for your life. God has important work for you to do. You are called by the Lord to live out your faith in good works of love and service to others.

The heavenly Father has chosen and called you to be his servant. Now, you seek to help others and to share the love of Christ with those who are hurting. This can happen in many different ways.

Often, the small things make all the difference. I'm not talking about big projects of social justice or campaigns to change the world. I'm talking about living in love and forgiveness each day. I'm talking about being a Christian in words and deeds.

Here, we simply seek to live out our faith in those everyday and ordinary situations we face, day after day. We try to deal with all those situations that can provoke and irritate us. We always treat other people with love and respect. We are merciful and compassionate.

Here, we follow the example of Jesus, who lived in total love, mercy and compassion. Moreover, when we begin to follow in the footsteps of Christ, we discover that we can let go of those ideas that God is angry with us, or that life has no purpose or meaning. We discover that we can make a difference in someone's life.

We can now joyfully share the love of God we have received. That is why you were redeemed in the first place. That is why God called you. God loves you and he wants you to live in love each day. He wants you to have an abundant life filled with joy and confidence.

We all know that life in this fallen world will always be filled with endless problems and heartache. We know things will happen to us that will test our faith. We know how hard life can be.

However, we also know that for those who love God, all things work together for good, for those who are called according to his purpose. We are God's workmanship, created in Christ Jesus to do good works, which God has prepared in advance for us to do. If God is for us, who can be against us?

Who shall separate us from the love of God revealed through the cross of Jesus? Shall trouble, problems, or the daily struggle of life ever separate us from God's love?

No, for we are convinced and we know that we are more than conquerors through him who loved us, and who gave himself for us.

We know beyond a shadow of a doubt, that neither death nor life, neither angels or demons, nor things present or things to come, no height or depth, or anything else in all of creation will be able to separate us from the love of God in Christ Jesus, our Lord.

We know! Amen!

SACRED & SECULAR: Matthew 18:1-20

Years ago, I saw a cartoon that showed a monk in a monastery. The monk was sitting at a big desk. He was filing papers by placing them in one of three wire baskets on his desk. The first basket was marked with a label that read, "Secular." The second carried the label, "Sacred." The third said, "Top Sacred."

Here is my point: We often think what we do inside this church is "sacred," and what we do outside the church is "secular." However, what we do outside the walls of this church is "top sacred." This is true because we live out our faith "out there," that is, in the secular world. We serve our Lord every single day of our life. We are 24-hours a day, 7-days a week Christians. We are God's people all the time. All of life is "Top Sacred."

Now it is true, we do fall into that trap of acting like part-time Christians. We come here to church once a week, and then we go back into our daily life, and we act and think just like everybody else. We blend in with the secular world. People cannot really tell that we are Christians at all.

From Monday through Saturday, there is nothing different about us. We live like an unbeliever, all during the week. Our faith is not even evident. No one can even tell that we are a believer in Christ.

That is like the college student who was talking with his friend about his upcoming summer job in the North Dakota oil fields. His friend said, "I wonder if you really know what you're letting yourself in for. That's a rough group of people up there, in the oil fields. How's that going to work out for you, since you are a Christian?"

Well, the summer passed, and the two friends met up again when college began. The one asked the other, "Well, how did you, a Christian, make out with that rough crowd?" "Oh," he answered, "I didn't really have any trouble. They never caught on that I was a Christian."

Today, our Lord calls for us to be people who live a sacred life in a secular world. We are called to be full-time Christians, people who totally dedicate themselves to God.

This means that we humble ourselves. We begin to serve others in true love and compassion. We become patient and caring people. We learn to control our anger; we are not mean to others. But we speak well of them, and put the best construction on everything.

Today, Jesus says, "You need to be converted. You need to turn around your life and become like a little child. Otherwise, you will never enter the kingdom of heaven. But whoever humbles himself like a child is the greatest in the kingdom of heaven."

Jesus says, "If you want to be great in the kingdom of God, you must humble yourself. You must be willing to be the least, the last, and the littlest of all." Therefore, that is how it is for all of us.

We need to humble ourselves like a little child. Such humility is the true attitude of a servant. This is the posture of Jesus himself. This is the way of God's kingdom, the way of the cross.

God's kingdom is also marked by avoiding temptation to sin. Our Lord says this is serious business. This is a life or death matter. We should not put ourselves in situations that lead to evil and wrongdoing.

Here, Jesus speaks of radical surgery. If something causes you to repeatedly sin, get rid of it. Remove that temptation. Cut it off and remove it from you. It is better to live without that temptation, than to be thrown into the fires of hell.

This is serious business. Living a life that is sacred means that you are willing to repent.

You are willing to turn your life around and make a new beginning. You make a daily confession of sin to God, and then, you resolve to live a new life through the power and help of the Holy Spirit.

But let's be honest and open. We are all prone to getting off track. We all stumble and fall. We repeatedly do what is wrong. We are not perfect people; we are sinners. We face that reality every single day.

However, the good news today is that our Lord Jesus has come into this world to redeem sinners who repeatedly fall. He has come to seek out and to save the lost.

Christ speaks of sheep that have gone astray, and he says that a good shepherd will always search for that one lost sheep. And that's how it is for us. We go astray and fall away from the Lord. But Jesus seeks us out and rescues the lost. It is the Father's will that none of his little ones should perish. God wants all people to be saved (and that includes you!)

This is precisely why the Son of God came into this fallen world. Even though he is true God in his essence and being, the Son was willing to humble himself and become our servant.

Even though he is true God, Christ took the posture of a lowly servant. The Son of God was willing to become the least, the last and the littlest of all, by dying on the cross for our sins.

Christ truly became the world's greatest sinner as he carried our burden. He suffered those fires of hell by taking our place and becoming our substitute.

But through this suffering and death, you have forgiveness and life. Through this humble sacrifice, you are brought into God's kingdom. The Lord now gives you a new beginning and a new chance at life.

Everything becomes holy and sacred for us. Everything in our life is wholly dedicated to our Lord who saved us. From now on, we constantly seek to serve others and to share the good news that our Savior has come.

This means that we should be willing to share the gift we have received. We give a witness to our Savior by how we live and act and treat others. We show we are Christians by how we conduct ourselves (especially Monday through Saturday).

The secular, unbelieving world should notice something different about us. Our words and deeds should always be a positive witness, proclaiming who we are, and what we believe. Our outward life should be plain evidence of our inner faith.

So many people today need to hear the good news of a compassionate Savior who deeply loves them. So many people today have no connection to God at all.

The truth is most Americans today are becoming more and more secular. We are all slowly becoming disconnected from God. We are losing touch with God's kingdom. Unbelief, atheism and skepticism are becoming the norm.

That is precisely why we are called to give a positive witness in a negative world. And we witness and testify not just in words (which certainly are important), but also by how we act and treat others.

That is why we need to be humble and patient people, real servants of God who truly care about others. We need to follow the way of Christ. We demonstrate every day how life in God's kingdom is far different from the way of the world.

A big example of how life in God's kingdom is completely different from our modern world is revealed in what Jesus says next. Our Lord tells us, "If your brother sins against you, go and tell him his fault, between you and him alone. Go and seek to be reconciled. Try to peacefully work this out. If he listens to you, you have gained a brother."

Notice how Jesus speaks of living in forgiveness and reconciliation. He calls for us to live in peace. If there is a problem between two people, they should seek a peaceful resolution. They need to strive for peace and reconciliation. Gently speak the truth in love. Try to put the best construction on everything. Seek to listen to others and try to understand their point of view.

This is certainly far different from the way of the world. The secular world says, "If your brother sins against you, go and get a lawyer. File a lawsuit. Retaliate. Strike back. Make them pay! Demand compensation."

However, Jesus says, "Live in peace with everyone. Seek reconciliation. Be willing to forgive." Jesus says, "Father, forgive them, for they know not what they do."

Now, to be sure, living such a Christian life is becoming more and more difficult nowadays. It is not easy living a sacred life in an increasingly secular world.

We also are caught up in our hurry-up, fast-paced society. We also fall prey to being rude and angry. We become impatient and frustrated. That is what happens when you live in a "quick fix, speed it up, I don't have time, I want it now" culture.

That is like the story of a woman who was shopping for cleaning supplies. The store was very busy, and she was waiting in a long checkout line. Her shopping cart was filled with a new broom and other cleaning supplies.

By the expression on her face, you could tell she was in a big hurry, and she was not happy about the slowness of the line. Then, the cashier had to ask for a price check.

The woman got angry, and said aloud so everyone could hear, "At this rate, I'll be lucky to get out of here before Christmas!" The cashier then replied, "Don't worry, ma'am. With that wind kicking up outside, and that brand new broom you have there, you'll be home in no time at all!"

As you can testify, such a scene is played out repeatedly in our world today. It is all too easy to get frustrated with waiting in long lines, or being stuck in traffic, or waiting for the service repair guy to show up (when he is already two hours late).

At best, life can be very challenging. Every day our faith is tested. We are tempted to sin and are put on the spot each day. Nevertheless, that is precisely why we need to remember that we belong to Christ. We are a part of God's kingdom. We follow the way of God's Messiah, the One who humbled himself to become our servant. And we need to realize that Christ is with us each and every day. The Lord is present in our life, 24-hours a day, 7-days a week, and 52-weeks a year.

Jesus says, "For where two or three gather in my name, there I am among them." "Lo, I am with you always." "I will never leave you or forsake you." "I will not leave you as orphans, I will come to you."

The Lord is with you! And Christ is with you to help you make that new beginning every morning. Each day, by God's grace, you can turn and become like a child. Each day, you can humble yourself and become a servant of the Lord.

Moreover, with God's help, we can all become patient, caring people. We are able to learn to live in forgiveness and reconciliation. We can let go of our anger and impatience. We can be at peace.

With God's help, you can now live a sacred life in a secular world. Amen!

ON THE RIGHT TRACK: Matthew 21:23-27

Do you know why the people of Israel wandered in the wilderness for 40 years? Because even back then, men would not stop and ask for directions.

Sometimes in life, you just have to stop and ask for directions. You got to have the right information, if you want to get on the right track. You have to have a reliable authority you can turn to, something you can absolutely trust. Otherwise, you're going to get lost.

Today, we how when Jesus entered the courtyard of the temple of Jerusalem to teach the crowds, the chief priests and the elders came up to him, and said, "By what authority are you doing all these things, and who gave you this authority?"

Jesus answered them, "I will also ask you a question. The baptism of John - where did it come from? Was it from heaven or from man?"

The leaders of the temple could not answer that one, so Jesus doesn't answer either. The Lord does not answer them because the leaders of Jerusalem ask in unbelief. Any answer given would never satisfy their stubborn unbelief and doubt. That is why they confront Jesus with the question, "By what authority are you doing all these things?"

You have to wonder, what exactly was Jesus doing that got them so upset? What did he do to make them so angry?

Well, the most recent thing that Jesus did was that he cleansed the temple in Jerusalem. He went into the temple courtyards and chased out all the moneychangers and all the buyers and sellers of merchandise. Christ cleanses the temple and restores it to its true purpose and function.

Then, he began to teach the crowds in the temple courts by proclaiming God's Word. That is when the leaders of Israel come up to him and ask, "By what authority are you doing all these things, and who gave you this authority?"

"Who gave you this authority?" That is the heart of the matter. Who is this Jesus of Nazareth? Who is this who cleanses God's temple? And who gave him this authority to do all these things?

There is a sense where Jesus does answer the question the leaders of Jerusalem ask. He specifically points them to John's baptism. He says, "The baptism of John, where did it come from?"

John was the great prophet sent by God to baptize and teach the people. John's mission was to prepare the way for the coming of God's Messiah. His baptism was for repentance and the forgiveness of sins.

Therefore, Christ asks the leaders, "If John was sent by God, why didn't you believe him? Why did you reject him? Why didn't you listen to him and receive his baptism?"

Our Lord points to John's baptism. Where did it come from? Was it something John made up? Is it from man? Or is it from God?

This is something many people wrestle with. They wonder, "Is all this Christianity stuff something somebody made up? Is the Christian faith something the church created and made up? Is it from man or from God?"

For example, consider the Bible. People wonder, "Is the Bible man-made? Is it really true? Is it reliable? Does it still have any authority for us nowadays or are we free to ignore and dismiss it?"

Many people today do have a low view of the Bible. They think it is outdated. They say the Bible just doesn't apply to modern life. It contains mistakes, errors and falsehood. It is just like any other book.

They say somebody just made up all these stories. It is fiction. The Old Testament is just a bunch of old campfire stories the people of Israel created, and the New Testament is the product of a group of delusional disciples.

However, we believe and teach that the Bible is what it claims to be - it is God's Word. The Bible comes from God, and his full authority stands behind every word. Therefore, the Scriptures are true and reliable, and they address the deepest human needs, now more than ever.

The Bible is God's message of hope and salvation to all of humanity. If we follow God's Word, we will be on the right track. We will have a reliable guide to help us in this crazy world.

In the very same way, baptism comes from God. Right before he ascended into heaven, the Risen Lord said to his disciples, "Go and baptize all nations." (That is worth repeating. Jesus specifically says, "Go and baptize. Go and do this." You see, this is his idea, not ours).

Similarly, in Holy Communion, Jesus says, "Do this in remembrance of me." He says, "Do this, remembering my sacrifice for you. Do this and receive my body and blood, given and shed for you."

Our Lord gives us baptism and Holy Communion so that we might receive his gift of life and love. Christ gives us his Word and

Sacraments, and he says, "Do this! Receive my Word and promise. Listen carefully to what I say to you through these means of grace."

The Bible, Holy Baptism and Holy Communion all speak the message of God's love for lost sinners. They all come from God, and the full power and authority of God stand behind them. They all declare God's free gift of love, mercy and grace.

The big problem, however, is that many people today reject God's love and grace. They disregard what Christ plainly tells us. In fact, most people today think they have the authority to reject God and his Word.

We think we have the authority to do whatever we want. We can play God and make up the rules as we go along. However, all of this is simply living in rebellion against the God who created us.

Such a rebellion only leads to confusion, chaos, and disorder. It leads to uncertainty and doubt. It leads to everyone doing whatever they think is fit. And if we try to live by our own ideas, we will end up getting lost and going the wrong way.

We need to follow the right authority – God's authority. Then, we will be on the right track. Then, we can know what life is really all about, why we are here, and what we should be doing.

It is evident that we live in a world filled with total confusion. People do not know where to turn for help, guidance and direction. We do not know who we can believe anymore. Fake news is everywhere. Disinformation and propaganda abound. Things are certainly getting crazy.

That is why people today feel trapped and helpless. This is what happens when we think we have the authority to live in rebellion against God and disregard what he says to us in his Word.

However, there is hope. Today, we see the full authority of Jesus Christ, the Son of God. He steps into our life and he calls for us to end our rebellion. He calls for us to turn away from our unbelief and doubt. Christ speaks his Word, and it is a Word of power and grace.

Our Lord is that Word of God made flesh. He has received authority from the Father to preach and teach God's Word to us. He has the authority to work miracles, to heal the sick, and to cast out demons. He has the authority to forgive sins. He has the authority to cleanse the temple and to restore God's creation.

The Son of God comes from heaven and he comes to rescue those who are trapped in sin and death. He goes to the cross and gives his life for the sins of the world. Jesus says, "I have the authority to lay down my life and take it up again. This command I have received from my Father."

Our salvation comes from God. This is God's work and not our own. It is God's gift and not from ourselves. There is nothing we could ever do to save ourselves.

That is precisely why the Son of God comes from heaven. He comes to heal the brokenness of our life. He comes to heal, to forgive and to restore. He cleanses our hearts and washes us clean with his blood. He saves us from sin and death, he bestows God's gift of salvation.

This gift of salvation is now given to us through Holy Baptism, through Holy Communion and through the Word of God.

God bestows his gifts through these means of grace, through Word and Sacrament. This is our certainty in times of uncertainty and confusion. Here is something reliable and true. When our world is falling apart, we know where we can turn.

We turn to Christ, the Son of God. We turn to the authority of his Word, his baptism, his Supper. The Word of Christ is the very power of God for the salvation for all who believe. His baptism is the miracle of a new birth, the Holy

Spirit's work of regeneration and renewal. The Lord's Supper is the very body and blood of Christ, given and shed for us.

Through these means of grace, sins are forgiven and life is freely bestowed. Here is something objective and true, something we can build our life upon, something we can implicitly trust with all of our heart and soul.

We turn to Christ and we find someone who can keep us on the right track. He says, "All authority in heaven and earth has been given to me. Therefore, go and make disciples of all nations, baptizing them in the name of the Father and of the Son and of the Holy Spirit."

Jesus says, "Go and learn my Word, listen to my teaching, follow the Scriptures and obey everything I have commanded you. And surely I am with you always, to the very end of the age."

Christ is with us each day and the Teacher shows us the way to go. Follow his authority and you will always be on the right track.

Follow Jesus in faith and love. Be in his Word. Worship the Lord every chance you get. Keep on believing and stay on the right track that leads all the way to eternal life. Amen!

FAMILY FEUD: Genesis 50:15-21

A Sunday School teacher was teaching her class about the importance of love within a family. She said that children should love their parents, and she illustrated her point by quoting the Fourth Commandment, "Honor your father and mother."

Then, she asked her class if there was a commandment that taught how brothers and sisters should treat each other. One boy who had several brothers immediately raised his hand and said, "Thou shalt not murder!"

Today, we look at the story of Joseph and his brothers. In that family, there was a lot of envy and jealousy. There was fighting and conflict; there was anger and hatred. There was a real lack of love.

Our text for today begins with the news that father Jacob has died. Suddenly, old fears return for the brothers. "What if Joseph holds a grudge against us, and pays us back for all the evil we did to him?"

This fear of retaliation was very real. You see, the brothers of Joseph had mistreated him terribly. They had always been jealous of him because he was the favorite son of Jacob. They couldn't stand the fact that their father considered Joseph to be his most special son.

Therefore, they came up with a bold plan to kill Joseph and hide his body. Then, they would tell their father that a wild animal had killed him. Imagine that! Murdering your own brother!

However, at the last minute, they changed their plan and sold Joseph as a slave to a caravan traveling down to Egypt. They sold him for 20 pieces of silver. And so, Joseph became a slave for many years. He suffered great evil down in Egypt.

Joseph was first resold to an Egyptian government official named Potiphar. Then, after a while, the wife of Potiphar falsely accused Joseph of trying to rape her. Because of this, Joseph would be arrested and taken away. He was unfairly condemned and imprisoned for three years.

After three years, Joseph rose from being a prisoner to the highest position in the government of Pharaoh. The turning point came when Joseph warned Pharaoh that a severe famine would strike the entire Middle East. Because of this warning, Pharaoh was able to prepare for the coming crisis.

When the famine struck, Egypt had plenty of food. In fact, people from all over the Middle

East began to travel down to Egypt to buy food. That included the brothers of Joseph. Jacob sent them down to Egypt to buy grain.

However, the brothers returned home with more than just grain. They returned with the amazing news that Joseph was alive, and he was now in charge of the entire land of Egypt. Joseph sent to have his father, all his brothers, and their entire families move down to Egypt. They had a great family reunion in the land of Goshen.

Now, years later, old fears come back to the surface after Jacob dies. "What if Joseph pays us back for what we did to him?" "What if he finally retaliates?" "What if he still holds a grudge?"

The brothers had an uneasy conscience, and it was a real fear they felt. Therefore, they sent a message to Joseph, saying, "Your father gave this command before he died, 'Please forgive the transgression of your brothers and their sin. Even though they did this great evil to you, forgive your brothers.'"

You can only wonder how many sleepless nights those brothers experienced in Egypt, wondering and worrying about what might happen to them. Within our own families, we often go through the same thing. We also have our family problems that give us sleepless nights and anxious days. We also deal with conflicts and fighting, with old fears and grudges. Family problems are nothing new, they go all the back to Cain and Abel.

Such conflict in the family gives us an uneasy conscience like those brothers had. We feel bad about the broken relationships we experience. It hurts us deeply; we often regret the way we treat others. We feel guilty over the hurtful things we may have said. We feel bad because of all the fighting and conflict going on, even if we are not directly involved.

So, what are we to do? We know that if we follow the way of our Lord Jesus, we are called to live in reconciliation and peace. We are called to forgive those who sin against us.

We do not seek vengeance or retaliate if someone offends us. When it comes to our personal relationships, Jesus tells us to turn the other cheek, to go the extra mile, and to be willing to forgive.

Our Lord teaches us that our heavenly Father has forgiven our huge debt of sin. Therefore, we should be willing to forgive others. We should forgive others, in the very same way God forgives us.

Such forgiveness is the glue that holds all relationships together. It is essential within any family. It is essential between a husband and wife, a parent and child, a brother and sister - essential for any relationship we find ourselves in. Forgiveness enables us to move on with our life and experience a little bit of peace and quietness.

We need to remember that we are all sinners. None of us is perfect. Moreover, we often act impulsively when someone does something bad to us. Our temper gets the best of us. We get angry. We seek to retaliate. That is when we do things we later regret. We hurt people, by what we say and do, and it makes us feel bad and uneasy afterward.

Here, we need to return to the cross and empty tomb. We need to look to the crucified Christ. We need to pray, "Father, forgive us our trespasses." We need to say, "Father, please forgive me all of my sins. And enable me to forgive others when they sin against me. And help me to forgive them from the heart."

Consider again the story of Joseph and his brothers. The brothers are afraid of Joseph retaliating now that their father is gone. Therefore, they now come to Joseph and fall down before him. They say, "Behold, we are your servants. Please forgive us for what we did to you."

And Joseph says to them, "Do not be afraid. You meant evil against me, but God meant it for good. Because of what happened to me, many people have been saved from the famine.

Even though you did evil to me, God was able to work good. Now, do not fear; I will provide for you and your families."

Now, think about what Joseph is really saying here. He says to his brothers, "You meant evil against me, but God meant it for good." That is an amazing statement!

In other words, Joseph is saying, "Yes, all those terrible things did happen to me after you sold me into slavery, that's true. But ultimately, God was able to use all of that to work the incredible good of saving many people from starvation. God's grace was at work in my life, I realize that now. God was able to bring salvation out of all this evil that occurred in my life."

What Joseph says here makes me think of what happened to our Lord Jesus. All these things that happened in the life of Joseph are a foreshadowing of what happened in the life of Christ. What happened to Joseph, happened to Jesus.

Our Lord suffered great evil, too, but God's grace was able to bring salvation to the entire world through the suffering of his Son. God was able to work good through all the bad things that happened to Jesus.

Just like Joseph, Christ would be the favorite Son of the Father. And the beloved Son of the

Father would be treated shamefully by his own brothers. He would be hated, rejected and betrayed by his own kin. He would be sold for 30 pieces of silver.

Jesus would be arrested and taken away. He would be falsely accused of many crimes and unfairly condemned. He would be beaten, whipped and abused. He would suffer and die on a Roman cross. Our Brother would be crucified. And he would suffer the greatest evil imaginable, enduring the punishment of hell and damnation.

However, just like Joseph, God was able to take that evil and bring incredible good out of it. God was able to work salvation for all people. "We know that in all things, God works for the good of those who love him, who have been called according to his purpose."

God's grace was at work in the life of Joseph, and most especially, God's grace was at work through everything that happened to Jesus. So too, God's grace is at work in our life as well.

God takes undeserving sinners like you and me, and he richly bestows his grace upon us. The Father says, "For the sake of my Son, I forgive you all of your sins. For the sake of your Brother, I remove all of your guilt. I take away all of your regrets and mistakes and failures. I wipe the slate clean. Your debt is forgiven!"

And so, what was true in the life of Joseph is true for us. Joseph forgave his brothers because he realized that God's grace had been at work in his life. And the same is true for us.

God's grace now motivates us to forgive those who sin against us. Because we are forgiven, we can now live in forgiveness each day. We can strive for reconciliation and peace when conflict occurs. We can follow the way of Christ.

Not far from New York City is a cemetery that has a unique grave. That grave has a headstone that has just one word inscribed on it, "FORGIVEN." There is nothing else on the headstone, no dates, no name, and no word of praise for the departed – just that one word, "FORGIVEN."

Now, think about that. What greater word could possibly be written on our own headstone? But perhaps to that one word, we could add another one, "FORGIVING."

"FORGIVEN" and "FORGIVING" always belong together. Just as we are taught to pray, "Forgive us our trespasses, as we forgive those who trespass against us." In other words, we are really praying, "God, forgive me my sins in the same way I am willing to forgive others." You see, being forgiven by God and being willing to forgive others always go hand in hand.

This petition of the Lord's Prayer reminds us we are called by God to share the incredible gift of forgiveness we have received from him. God has forgiven all of our sins from his heart, and we should be willing to forgive others in the same way.

To be sure, this is not an easy thing to do. However, with God's help, we can make an effort to turn away from our anger and resentment. We can learn to grow in love and compassion.

Is there some conflict in your life? Do you carry a grudge against someone? Do you argue and fight with members of your family? Is there someone at work that you are always mad at?

Do you have a strained relationship with a spouse, a child, a parent, a brother or sister? Do you have a hard time controlling your anger? Do you wish you could live in peace and harmony with others?

If so, then let the amazing grace of God touch your heart today. Receive God's gift. Embrace the cross and resurrection of Jesus. Learn to follow the way of God. Pray the Lord's Prayer with faith and understanding as you seek reconciliation with others.

Then, the Risen Lord will truly change your heart. The Holy Spirit will open your eyes to see the wondrous power of the Father's love.

You will discover once again that Christ died and rose again for you, and he wants you to have a life filled with peace and quietness and harmony with others. Let God's grace motivate you to love and accept others in the very same way God has loved and accepted you. Then, you will discover what Joseph learned after all those long years in Egypt.

You will realize that God is control of all things, and God is always at work in your life to bring you closer to him and closer to the likeness of Christ.

You will discover that when you follow God's ways, all things really do work together for good, for those who have been called according to God's purpose. Amen!

DON'T GO 'ROUND HUNGRY: 1 John 4:1-11

Years ago, there was a cult in San Diego named, "Heaven's Gate." This cult made the headlines when 39 people committed suicide together in a single house.

They thought there was a spaceship traveling in the wake of the Hale-Bopp comet, and so, they killed themselves to transport their souls to "the next level," to a better life onboard the UFO. Perhaps you remember the pictures of the house and the people.

You have to wonder, how in the world could anyone believe in all that UFO stuff, and believe in it so strongly, that you would take your own life? How could they put their faith in something that is so weird and far-out?

The answer is that you would be surprised at what some people believe in. There are many people in the world today who will believe in anything, if it can give them some kind of hope. They will follow a false prophet and believe all kinds of weird teaching, if it can give them comfort and hope.

Listen to what the Apostle John says in our reading, "Beloved, do not believe every spirit, but test the spirits to see whether they are from God, because many false prophets have gone out into the world."

"Test the spirits," says John. "Check to see whether these spirits come from God or not." In other words, not everything spiritual is necessarily from God. Not every religion is true. There are many false prophets out there. You have to test them to separate truth from falsehood.

Today, John tells us how we can find the truth we are looking for. And let's be honest – all of us are searching for the truth. We all are seeking for answers to life's deepest questions. We all are seeking hope, comfort, and the promise of a better life.

Consider again the people of "Heaven's Gate." These were not stupid people. They were not poor or uneducated. But rather, they were well off and very well educated. They were men and women who had good jobs, and who lived in one of the most affluent, exclusive neighborhoods of San Diego. They were healthy, wealthy and had every advantage in life.

Yet, something was missing in their life. They still lacked something. Even though they were well off materially, there was an emptiness in their hearts. There was a hole in their soul. They had a deep, spiritual hunger.

Without a doubt, there is a deep void in modern life. Despite all the advantages we enjoy in this modern world, there is an emptiness inside of us. We feel hollow inside. We sense something is missing.

People try to fill that void in many ways. Some people seek power and fame. Some put their hope in technology, computers and science. Some try to accumulate wealth and possessions. Others devote themselves to sports and entertainment. Some try alcohol or drugs.

But still, even if we have everything the world has to offer, it never seems quite enough. Something is still missing. We are never quite happy. We never feel really safe, secure, and content. We continue to feel restless and adrift.

This reminds me of the old joke about a millionaire who stipulated in his will that he be buried in his favorite car, a $90,000.00 Rolls Royce Silver Cloud. When the millionaire died, they had his funeral, and they buried him exactly as he wished.

After the service, two cemetery workers were shoveling the last bit of dirt onto the now buried car. When they were done, one guy turned to the other one and said, "Man, that's really living!"

That is often how we think. We may think real life can be found in wealth, possessions, power, and fame. However, all those things are so uncertain and subject to change. They are only temporary, at best. That is why they cannot satisfy our spiritual hunger. We need something better, something more lasting, something permanent.

Listen again, to what John says, "Beloved, do not believe every spirit, but test the spirits. By this you will know the Spirit of God - every spirit that confesses that Jesus Christ has come in the flesh is from God, and every spirit that does not confess Jesus is not from God."

John points us to the ultimate test. He points us to Christ, the Son of God. He is the One who has come in the flesh. He is the truth of God made flesh. He is the incarnate Son of God who comes directly from the Father to show us the answers we are looking for.

Jesus says, "I am the vine; you are the branches. Whoever abides in me will bear much fruit. But apart from me, you can do nothing." Christ says, "Peace I leave with you; my peace I give you. I do not give to you as the world gives. Do not let your hearts be troubled, and do not be afraid." Our Lord points to himself as the source of true life and peace.

Christianity is something far different from any other religion. This is not some theory or philosophy. This is not some program or 10 steps to success. Christianity is a person. Christianity is "God made flesh." Christianity is Jesus of Nazareth.

He is the Way, the Truth and the Life. He fills the emptiness inside us. He gives us the answers we are looking for. He feeds our spiritual hunger. He bestows upon us lasting peace. The Son of God gives us his love.

And I think that is what people today are really looking for. They want the certainty of knowing that they are loved and accepted by God. They want the certainty of knowing a better life exists. And they want to know that God himself has done everything necessary for our complete salvation.

John says, "This is how God showed his love among us - God sent his only Son into the world, so that we might live through him. This is love, not that we have loved God, but that he loved us, and sent his Son to be the atoning sacrifice for our sins."

That word, "atoning," is important. It means that Christ paid the ultimate price. He suffered that punishment we deserve. He took upon himself God's judgment against our sins. That is what happened on the cross. Christ took upon himself all the sin and evil of this entire world.

That is how much God loved you. The Father loved you so much, that he gave his Son to be that perfect and final atoning sacrifice for you. Jesus told his disciples, "The Son of Man did not come to be served, but to serve, and to give his life as a ransom for many."

The Son of Man does what we could never do on our own. He dies our death and deals with our sin problem. He reconciles us to the Father and restores our spiritual connection to the source of all true life. "I am the vine and you are the branches."

The way to a better existence is now wide open for you. In Christ, you have the promise of something better than what you have right now. This is the hope of a permanent life of perfect health and happiness.

You have this hope in Jesus, and this hope fills the emptiness inside. Christ is the Bread of Life that satisfies our deepest spiritual hunger. He is the answer we are all looking for.

When I was a kid growing up in Texas, the convenience stores and gas stations had these vending machines from a snack company called, "Tom's." These were those big, shiny, vending machines, with those old-fashioned handles you would have to pull to get your snack.

Across the front of every "Tom's" vending machine, there was a big mirror with a slogan in big red letters across it. The slogan said, "Don't Go 'Round Hungry!" As you stood there before the machine, you would see your face in the mirror, and the words, "Don't Go 'Round Hungry!" across your image.

I was always struck by that. The message really stuck in your mind. "Don't go around hungry!" Indeed, why would anyone want to go around hungry, when there were delicious snacks, right in front of you?

Here is my point: I think we should print that message on the front of every Bible, "Don't Go 'Round Hungry!" I mean, why go around spiritually hungry, when you can satisfy your hunger with the Word of God? Why be hungry, when you have the Bread of Life, right before you?

What you need to do is simply take up the Bible and prayerfully read it. Start with the First Letter of John. Then, read Peter's First Letter. Explore the Gospel of Mark. Try James. Then, read some other book that interests you. Continue to read and ponder the message of the Scriptures. Read as the Holy Spirit leads you.

Each day, feed upon the Word of God. Discover the incarnate Son of God. Receive his message with an open heart and you will then experience something that really satisfies your deepest hunger. You will find what you are searching for.

John says, "We have seen and testify that the Father has sent his Son to be the Savior of the world." "In this, the love of God was made manifest among us, that God sent his only Son into the world, so that we might live through him." "If anyone acknowledges Jesus is the Son of God, God lives in him and he lives in God."

Here, John is giving us something certain, true and reliable. John is pointing us to God's love in Jesus. We don't need to run around and chase after what the world may offer us. We don't need to go 'round hungry. We don't need to be unhappy, uncertain and restless. The Living Bread has come down from heaven, and he feeds our hungry heart.

Therefore, feed upon the Bread of Life. Put Christ at the center of your everyday life. Attend worship and receive his gifts.

Then, you can rejoice and give thanks every day, knowing that God loves you deeply and he accepts you as his very own. Don't go around hungry anymore. Amen!

THE DUMPSTER OF GOD: John 2:13-25 & Exodus 20:1-21

Every so often, when I drive through my neighborhood, I will notice the presence of a dumpster in someone's driveway. That is usually a sure sign that someone is moving. Someone is going through that painful process of packing up all their possessions so they can move to a new home.

Moving can be a traumatic experience. It is probably one of the hardest things you can do. The packing process is hard work, and I especially find it difficult to decide what to keep or what to throw away.

I am from the school of thought that says, "It's best to hang on to something - you never know when you might need it." My wife thinks differently. She says, "If you're not going to use it, throw it away." However, I find it hard to throw things away. (You should see my basement and garage.)

However, I have noticed something. Once you start throwing stuff away, it becomes easier. There is a definite satisfaction to be found in totally cleaning house. Once you get started, it is kind of fun to throw stuff away.

You start thinking, "Why did I keep all these old magazines? Do I really need these old tennis shoes? What am I going to do with this broken lawnmower? Do I really need a twenty-year-old bed frame? Why am I keeping all these empty coffee cans?"

And especially when you rent a dumpster, you can get carried away. After you finish your cleaning up, you suddenly realize that the dumpster is only half-full.

That is when you say to yourself, "Well, I'm paying all this money to rent this thing. It's only half-full. I might as well try and fill it up!" Then, you start searching for more stuff to throw away. You start walking all around the house, looking for something to throw in the dumpster because you want to fill it up.

There is definitely a satisfaction to be found in cleaning house. Sometimes you just have to let go of all that junk and make a fresh start. You need to set things in order and make a new beginning.

In today's reading, we see how Jesus cleans house. Our Lord cleanses the temple in Jerusalem. He cleans house so that God's temple can be restored to its true purpose and function. (You should note that there are two accounts of Jesus clearing out the temple in Jerusalem: This one in John 2, and the one that happened after Palm Sunday. It would appear that Jesus did this cleansing a couple of times, maybe more. That would ring true, since the merchants would probably bring all their junk right back into the temple courts after Jesus left town. This appears to have been an ongoing problem for the temple.)

Today, John tells us that Jesus and his disciples are in Jerusalem for the big Passover celebration. People from all over the world would travel to Jerusalem for the great festival. They would come to worship at the temple and to offer their sacrifices.

In addition, since these people could not bring their own animals with them, they would buy animals in Jerusalem to offer as sacrifices. They also would have their money changed into the local currency, so they could pay the temple tax and make their offerings. So far, so good.

The problem was that many of the local merchants took advantage of the situation. They actually moved their business into the courtyards of the temple itself. The house of God took on an almost "State Fair" appearance. It became filled with moneychangers, noisy vendors and pens of various animals. Under these circumstances, it became difficult for anyone to think about worship and prayer.

No wonder the sight of all of this made Jesus angry. He made a whip out of cords, and drove out the animals and the vendors. He overturned the tables of the moneychangers, scattering their coins. And to those who were selling pigeons, he said, "Take these things away! Do not make my Father's house into a house of trade."

You see, the temple in Jerusalem was the place where God the Father had promised to meet his people. God was truly present in his sanctuary – God himself dwelt there, in the holy of holies (the inner room of the temple).

Therefore, the people of Israel came to worship God in the temple. They came to hear his Word proclaimed by the priests, to offer their sacrifices and prayers, and to receive the blessing of the Lord. But the merchants had filled God's house with all this junk – junk that prevented the people from truly worshipping the Lord and receiving his gifts.

That is why Christ was so concerned about cleansing the temple in Jerusalem. This temple was God's house, God's sanctuary, God's dwelling place.

The same is true for us today, but in a different way. The difference is Jesus. We see that in what follows after the Lord drives out all the merchants, business people, vendors and moneychangers.

The authorities in the temple confront him and say, "Who do you think you are? Give us a sign to prove your authority to do these things." Jesus points to himself and says, "Destroy this temple, and in three days I will raise it up."

The authorities say, "Hold on! Wait a minute. It took us over 40 years to build this temple complex. How could you raise it up in three days?" But John tells us that Jesus was referring to the temple of his body. Our Lord was referring to his bodily resurrection. That would be God's sign to the entire world that Jesus truly is the Messiah, God's punch line, so to speak.

The Easter resurrection confirms that Jesus of Nazareth is the promised Messiah. And after his bodily resurrection, the current temple in Jerusalem would no longer be necessary. Jesus has now become the new temple of God. He is Emmanuel, God dwelling with us in the flesh.

Christ is now our temple, the true sanctuary of God, the holy of holies, the Ark of the Covenant, our mercy seat. He is the place where God now meets his people.

That is why when our Lord rose from the dead, the entire temple system of animal sacrifices and the priesthood became no longer necessary. Something better has now come, the fulfiller of all of God's promises in the Old Testament has arrived – Jesus the Messiah. He is now God's temple system, par excellence. (He is also our High Priest, the perfect and final Lamb of God, and the true Sabbath. In fact, Christ fulfills and completes all the Old Testament worship practices and requirements. See the Book of Hebrews to learn more.)

In addition, going one step further, this whole concept of God's temple is now expanded to all believers. Not only is Jesus the true temple of God, but God declares we now share in this reality. We, too, are God's temple. God dwells in our hearts through the Holy Spirit. Paul says to the Corinthians, "Do you not know that you are God's temple and that God's Spirit lives in you? Your body is a temple of the Holy Spirit."

Therefore, you are God's temple! That is pretty amazing, right? But, of course, this leads us to the question, "What kind of shape is your temple in?"

When Jesus came to Jerusalem, he cleaned house because he found the temple there was cluttered up with all kind of junk and garbage.

So, how is your temple? Is it filled up with all this stuff you really need to throw away? Is there some junk in your life that prevents you from worshipping the Lord? Is there some garbage you would like to get rid of?

In Exodus 20, we find the Ten Commandments, the great summary of God's law. As we reflect upon this Word of God, we have to confess that our life is cluttered up with the garbage of sin. These commandments remind us how we fall short of the glory of God.

If we stop for a moment, and take a spiritual inventory, we will realize our true condition. If we walk through our house and use these commandments as a guide, we can realize that we need to do some housecleaning. Ask yourself:

+Do I put God first? Is God the most important person in my life?

+Do I honor God's name by how I use it? Or is God's name only a curse word that I use for profanity?

+Do I remember the Sabbath principle and make time each week for worship and hearing God's Word?

+Do I honor my parents? Do I show respect to those in authority over me?

+Do I have a problem with my temper? Am I constantly fighting with my spouse? Am I harsh with my children?

+Do I spend a lot of time arguing and complaining at work?

+Do I honor God with my sexuality and respect the sanctity of marriage?

+Do I have a problem with greed and materialism? Am I obsessed with money and financial issues?

+Am I honest in my dealings with others?

+Do I tell lies to cover up my actions?

+Do I bear a grudge and refuse to forgive those who sin against me?

+Am I a selfish person? Am I obsessed with gratifying all of my desires and whims?

What shape is your temple in? Is your heart filled up with a bunch of junk, trash and garbage? If we are honest, we have to confess that our life is a big mess. We need to clean house.

The good news today is that the Messiah has come to do exactly that. He comes to clean house. He brings his dumpster, and he parks it right in the driveway of our life. Then, he cleanses our hearts and gives us a fresh start.

The truth is everyone needs such a fresh start. We need to just finally throw this rotten junk away. We need to get rid of our guilt and bad feelings, and throw away everything that is wrong in our life. Just let go of all that garbage and throw it into the dumpster.

When this happens, we experience the cleansing power of the Messiah. He makes a whip of cords and fiercely drives out everything that clutters up the temple of our heart. He takes all this junk to the dumpster of his cross.

That's right - the cross is the dumpster of God. When Jesus hung upon the cross, he received all the sin, garbage, and rotten evil of this entire world. He carries all of the trash we ever created down into the dumpster of his death. In this way, our trash is taken away. Our guilt is removed. We are now cleansed.

The cross of Jesus is that powerful because this is the Son of God who suffers and dies for us. God himself does what we could never do. That is why Jesus points to himself and says. "Destroy this temple, and in three days I will raise it up." Our Lord points to himself, and he says, "This is how you can clean up your life. I am the way."

Because of what Christ has done for us, we are now God's restored temple, the place where the Holy Spirit dwells. The Holy Spirit now lives in you! And the Spirit of God will help you to keep the temple of your heart clean. However, you need to remember this is a lifelong process. It is an ongoing restoration project where each day we return to the cross and resurrection of Jesus. Each day, we confess our sins and receive absolution.

Each day, we pray, "Forgive us our trespasses." Each day, the Holy Spirit enables us to move forward with this process of cleaning house and setting things in order. When this happens, we grow in our faith and obedience to God's Word. We bring our life closer to the Ten Commandments. Our life becomes more Christ-like. But again, this is a lifelong process.

That is why it is so important to stay connected to worship. We need to hear the gospel over and over again. We need to hear that message of God's dumpster, the cross of Jesus, repeatedly. We need to receive the cleansing power of God at work in our hearts. We need the Holy Spirit.

Today is a great opportunity to do some spiritual housecleaning. Christ is that cleansing power of God made flesh. And because of him, we can now clean house and begin to live each day in God's renewing love and grace. So, let's get busy and fill up that dumpster. Amen!

IT ISN'T FAIR! Matthew 20:1-16

The movie "Amadeus" is the story of the great musical genius, Wolfgang Amadeus Mozart. The movie portrayed Mozart as a rather eccentric guy, but a very gifted musician and composer.

Another composer, the devout Antonio Salieri, despised Mozart and considered him immature, arrogant and obnoxious. He thought to himself, "Why should Mozart be such a gifted musician, when he doesn't deserve it?"

After all, Salieri thought he was special. So, why shouldn't God give him success and fame instead of Mozart? After all, he was a better person and he certainly deserved it.

Finally, in a moment of despair, Salieri feels that God has forsaken him, so he removes his crucifix down from the wall, and he burns it. In the end, Salieri could not live with God's grace. He wanted fairness and justice. He wanted what he thought he had worked for and earned.

Many times in our life, we also think, "It isn't fair!" We also complain that God is not being fair with us. We don't get what we deserve or have earned.

The Bible is full of examples of unfair situations. God chose Jacob, a deceiver and cheat over his older brother, Esau. God chose a scrawny shepherd boy, David, above his stronger and older brothers. Jesus chose to have dinner with a notorious crook named Zacchaeus, instead of the religious leaders of Jericho.

What about the feast that was prepared for the prodigal son, when he returned home after wasting all his inheritance? Nothing was given to the older son who had worked so hard while his brother ran away to have a good time.

What about the thief on the cross? After a life of crime, he made a last minute confession of faith and the Lord promised that he would be saved. That hardly seems fair.

Do you get the picture? A theme that runs through the entire Bible is that the last will be first and the first will be last. Our reading for today is a classic example of this.

Jesus tells us about a farmer who had a bumper crop and hired some people to work for him. Some clocked in at sunrise, some at morning, some at lunchtime and some at the afternoon coffee break. The farmer even hired some just an hour before everyone quit for the day.

Everyone was just happy to be working, but things changed when it came time to be paid. Those who had worked all day received the same pay as those who had worked for just one hour.

This hardly seems fair. Why should these latecomers receive the exact same pay as the regular workers? These latecomers had been lazing around the marketplace for most of the day. They had done nothing to deserve the same pay as those who had worked all day.

This story of Jesus makes no sense. However, that was his intent. Christ is giving us a parable about God's grace. Grace cannot be calculated like a day's wages. Grace is not about finishing last or first. It is not something we work to earn; it is not our paycheck. Grace is not based on the merit system - it is a free gift given by God.

This point is made crystal clear through the farmer's response. "Listen, friend," he answered one of the workers who complained, "I have not cheated you. I am not being unfair. After all, you agreed to do a day's work for one silver coin. Now, take your pay, and go home. Don't I have the right to do what I want with my own money? Or, are you envious because I am so generous?"

The farmer didn't cheat anyone. They had all agreed to work for a set wage. Everyone got what was promised. The problem was not with the farmer – the problem was with the workers. Some of the workers could not accept the fact that the boss had the right to be generous to whomever he wished. However, it all sounds so unfair, and humanly speaking, it is.

What the Lord Jesus is trying to tell us today is that if God were strictly fair, he would indeed pay us according to what we deserve. And that is bad news because all of us would end up in hell.

The truth is we deserve to be punished and condemned for our sins. That is our paycheck. We have earned God's wrath and punishment. We deserve hell and eternal damnation. That would be our wages. "The wages of sin is death." That's the bad news.

The good news today is that God doesn't deal with us according to what we deserve. God doesn't treat us according to the merit system.

Our God is generous, full of mercy and compassion. He does not treat us according to what we deserve. And our God is gracious because of who he is and not because of who we are.

The truth is we are fallen sinners, rebels against God. Sin takes control of what we say, do and think. Our words and actions reveal what is inside of us. We have a real problem with anger, hatred, pettiness and complaining all the time. We constantly rebel against God and disregard his Word. However, the owner of the vineyard does not give up on us. He continues to love us.

In love, the Father sends his Son, Jesus Christ, to suffer and die for us. The Son of God takes our place and dies on the cross for us. He is punished instead of us. And this is terribly unfair.

The Son of God is the Sinless One and yet he dies for the sin of everyone else. He was holy but he became a sinner. He was innocent but he became guilty. He was first but he became last. He was greatest but he became least. He was the highest and yet he became the lowest. This death of Jesus on the cross was totally unfair, but that is God's grace at work.

Think of it this way: When we go shopping, all our purchases are added up at the cash register. Then, we are told how much we have to pay. If God did that with our life, we would be in trouble. If God got out his cash register and added up all the sins we ever committed, all our sins of thought, word and deed, we would be lost. We would perish in the depths of hell.

However, God does not calculate what we deserve. He is generous and forgiving. He takes that cash register and he nails it to the cross. Christ pays the price for us. He is the one who perishes in the depths of hell. He pays the price with his innocent suffering and bitter death. The first became last, so that the last might become first.

That is the good news today. God the Father declares, "For the sake of my Son, I forgive you all of your sins. That is my gift to you! Because of Jesus, you are now first in my heart. I love you and I forgive you. You are mine, forever!"

You see, that is grace. That is God's free gift to you. One final point before we end. God's forgiveness toward us is totally undeserved. There are no strings attached and no conditions are added. Therefore, since God has so graciously forgiven us, we are now called to be gracious and merciful to others in the very same way.

God is generous with his forgiveness and we are called to practice the exact same kind of forgiveness in our daily life. This means I stop saying, "It isn't fair!" I stop all my arguments about who is right or wrong. I overcome that part of me that feels hurt and wronged. I conquer that need to get revenge and get even. I rise above that part of me that wants to put conditions on the one whom I am asked to forgive.

Certainly, this is a very hard thing for us to do. We all have ingrained in us the merit system that says, "You get what you deserve. Therefore, it is only fair that I get you back if you do something to me."

However, remember how God has treated you. God is generous with his forgiveness. You do not deserve this gift. The last have become first. The undeserving are forgiven. We graciously welcomed back into God's kingdom. That is exactly why we share God's gift by practicing forgiveness in our daily life.

C.S. Lewis says, "I never find forgiveness easy and rarely do I find it completely satisfying. Nagging injustices remain and the old wounds still cause pain. I have to approach God repeatedly, yielding to him the residue of what I thought I had committed to him long ago. I do so because the Lord's Prayer makes a clear connection here. God forgives my debts, as I forgive my debtors. The reverse is also true. Only by living in the stream of God's grace will I find the strength to respond with grace toward others."

That is so true. We need to let God's grace stream in and flow into our lives. Grace just needs to fill our hearts to the brim. Then, we can learn to live in reconciliation and peace.

Again, this is a difficult task for us to do. It is hard, and the more we realize this, the more we come to appreciate the gift of God's grace. But that's how it is in God's kingdom.

The more we realize our weakness, the more we appreciate the power of God. The more we struggle in our life, the greater is the strength of God. The more we confess our weakness, the stronger we become in Christ. God says, "My grace is sufficient for you. My power is made perfect in weakness."

Listen: God's grace is a powerful gift. It can change your heart and renew your soul. It can create a right spirit within you. It can make you to be a different person, someone who is now willing to live in grace, forgiveness, reconciliation and peace. You can let go of your anger, resentment and frustration. You can stop complaining that life is not fair.

You have received God's gift. Be at peace. Grace has been bestowed. Now pass on that gift to others. Go now and live in love and reconciliation. Go and follow the way of God's kingdom. Learn to forgive even as Christ has forgiven you. Amen!

POWER FAILURE: Mark 9:14-29

Several years ago, in early fall, we had both Hurricane Irene and the "October Snowstorm." Both of those events caused massive power failures. Most of the trees still had their leaves on them, and as a result, many trees and power lines came down.

The lights went out and we all sat in darkness. I'm sure you remember dealing with the power outages, and all the inconvenience of not having electricity. A long-term power failure means that you not only lose electricity, but you also lose your water. Then, you're really stuck.

After Hurricane Irene came through, I remember the frustration of realizing that I did not have enough batteries in the house. Without flashlights, you have to rely on candles. And candles are a poor substitute for a bright and clear light.

In today's reading, we see how some of the disciples had a power failure. They were unable to help a man who had a demon-possessed son. The lights went out for them and they sat in the dark. They were frustrated and confused. In the end, their problem was a basic lack of faith.

To set the stage for our story today, we need to realize that Jesus had just been up on the Mount of Transfiguration with three of his disciples, Peter, James, and John. It was a tremendous experience for those disciples, as they saw Jesus being transfigured before them.

The bright and powerful light of God's glory was clearly revealed. The face and body of Christ shined with a brilliant light, and his glory and power were revealed. Here was a brief glimpse of the true divinity of the Son of God.

Afterward, when they came down the mountain, they arrived in the dark valley below and saw the other disciples surrounded by an agitated crowd. The disciples were arguing with the people about something. It was a chaotic scene. Therefore, Jesus asks what the argument is about.

A man in the crowd steps forward, and says, "Teacher, I brought my son to you because he has an evil spirit that makes him mute. Whenever the spirit seizes him, it throws him down, and he foams at the mouth, grinds his teeth, and becomes rigid. So, I asked your disciples to cast it out, but they were not able to."

In frustration, Jesus responds by saying, "O faithless generation, how long am I going to be with you? How long do I have to put up with you?"

This is a surprising response. It is totally unexpected, but it shows an interesting insight into the true humanity of Christ. Even though he is true God (we saw that briefly on the Mount of Transfiguration), Jesus was also a real human being like us, subject to frustration and disappointment. Christ had real human emotions, just like us.

And often, we see how Jesus is frustrated by his disciples' lack of faith and understanding. Those guys just had such a hard time comprehending what Jesus was all about. "You of little faith, why did you doubt?"

Therefore, I think these words of Christ are not aimed at the father of the sick boy, but at the disciples. It is as if the Lord is saying, "Come on, guys! How long is it going to take for you to get a handle on what I'm talking about?"

The disciples were totally baffled and confused by what had just happened to them. They were filled with doubt and uncertainty. That is why they were not able to cast out this evil spirit.

It wasn't that long ago that the Lord had given the 12 disciples power and authority over demons. Jesus had just sent them out on a special mission trip. He sent them into the nearby towns and villages, and they went forth and not only proclaimed the gospel, but they also successfully drove out demons.

It was evident the disciples had received the power of Christ. However, in this one case, they had a power failure, and they were not able to drive the demon from this boy.

Afterward, they asked Jesus privately, "Why couldn't we drive it out?" And the Lord replied, "This kind cannot be driven out by anything, but prayer."

It seems like the disciples had taken the power of prayer for granted. They no longer totally depended upon the Lord Jesus. They no longer prayed, "Lord, help me to share your gift of deliverance and rescue; help me to live in your power and light; help me to follow you by faith."

Perhaps the disciples started to rely on their own power and strength. Perhaps they thought that they were now spiritually self-sufficient. Maybe they thought that they could move on beyond Jesus to other matters.

Many Christians seem to think that way. They think once you are baptized and confirmed, then that's good enough. They think, "I don't need to pray anymore. I don't need worship or Holy Communion. I don't really need Christ anymore. I am good to go." However, we know that is not true.

Martin Luther once said, "This life is not righteousness, but growth in righteousness; not health, but healing; not being, but becoming; not rest, but exercise. We are not yet what we shall be, but we are growing toward it. The process is not yet finished, but it is going on; this is the not the end, but it is the road; all does not yet gleam with glory, but all is being purified by grace."

What Luther means is that our spiritual life is an ongoing process. We need to stay connected to Jesus Christ, the Son of God. We cannot unplug our spiritual life from the power source of his cross and resurrection. We cannot drop off the grid and expect that everything will fine without the Lord's presence in our life.

We need to continually grow stronger in our faith. We need to grow in the grace and knowledge of the Lord. We need to rely solely upon the power of Christ, and not ourselves. If we try to rely on our own power, we are going to end up like the disciples who failed.

Those doubting disciples were unable to help the father with the sick boy. And when the disciples had their power failure, even the father began to have his doubts. Even after

Jesus arrives on the scene, he still is uncertain and confused.

Jesus asks the father, "How long has this been happening to him?" He replied, "From childhood. It often casts him into the fire and the water to try to destroy him. However, if you can do anything, have compassion on us. Lord, help me!"

Then, Jesus said to the boy's father, "All things are possible for the one who believes." Immediately, the father cried out, "I believe; help my unbelief!"

The father cries out, "Lord, I do believe, but help me overcome my doubt and unbelief." You see, this man was struggling with his faith; he was having his own power failure. Like the disciples, he was having a hard time in his spiritual life.

This happens to us as well. We often struggle and stumble about in our spiritual life. We sense that our faith is not what it should be. Questions and doubts plague our thoughts.

We experience a power failure, and the lights go out. And this can happen to anyone. Paul says, "If you think you are standing firm, be careful that you don't fall."

But today, we see how the Son of God enters into our confusion and uncertainty. He comes down the Mount of Transfiguration and meets the disheartened disciples and the father of the sick boy.

Our Lord sees this chaotic situation, and he commands the evil spirit to come out and never return. And the spirit has to obey. The boy is immediately healed and delivered from his affliction.

For this is the Son of God in human flesh. He does not have any power failure. And Christ not only has incredible power, but he also has great compassion.

The Lord is there to help you in your hour of need. Christ speaks his Word of power and release, and healing occurs. He shines the light of his love upon you and the darkness flees. He speaks his Word and trapped people are set free. He commands even the evil spirits and they have to obey.

Here, we see the power of Christ so clearly revealed. He does what the disciples could not do. And the same holds true for us. We are unable to rescue ourselves, but Jesus saves us. We are unable to take away our guilt and past, but he bestows forgiveness. We are unable to defeat death, but the Son of God wins the victory over death and the grave.

Our Lord does all this through his cross and resurrection, and his true power is revealed most clearly through his sacrificial love. Christ willingly suffered for us, and that is the greatest power of all.

Christ bears our burden, as he hangs on the cross. He even prays, "Father, forgive them, for they know not what they do." Our Lord prays for us from the cross, and in this way, he drives out the demons that plague us. ("For this kind cannot be driven out by anything, but prayer".)

Jesus Christ sets us free from all sin and evil. He totally defeats the devil. He removes the sting of death. He delivers us from the darkness of sin. And he does all this through the power of his love. His power just lights up our soul with a brilliant light.

We know all of this is true, but somehow, just like the father of the sick boy, we still struggle in our faith. We know Christ has the power to help us, but we still doubt. We just have such a hard time believing God's power is really at work in our life. We also say, "Lord, I believe; help my unbelief! Lord, I'm having such a hard time believing."

As we once again struggle in our faith, the lights suddenly go out, and it seems as if God's power has failed us once more. We are stuck in yet another power outage. Surrounded by darkness, we reach for our flashlights and discover our batteries are dead yet again.

However, you need to remember that the power of God never goes out; it never fails. It is our faith in God that fails. The power of God is always there. The power of his love revealed through the cross of Jesus never goes out.

This basic principle is true, even for our power and electric companies. Technically, the electric power never goes out – what goes out is the local power grid, that is, your neighborhood's transmission system.

Even during Hurricane Irene and the "October Snowstorm," the electrical power was still on. The power never went out. The problem was that we fell off the power grid when our local power lines went down. Our connection to the main overall power source was broken. That is what the power crews were working to reestablish. (And I'm sure you remember how some neighborhoods got their power back before others. In fact, some towns had to wait for several weeks for power to be restored).

But my point is that you don't have to sit in the dark, day after day. Christ wants to reestablish your power lines and get you reconnected. He wants to bring you back onto his grid. Christ wants for you to live in the power of his love every day.

Our Lord wants to shine the light of his love upon you. He wants to show mercy to you in your time of need. He wants to forgive your sins and give you eternal life. He wants to be the Lord of your life. And, as we once again reconnect with Christ, we discover that we are now able to have faith. We can trust that God's power is at work in our life (even if it may not seem that way to us at the moment).

We can discover that God truly is in control of our life. "All things are possible for the one who believes." Faith is able to weather the storm. But the key is to stay connected to God's power grid through regular worship, prayer and Holy Communion. Stay connected to the cross and resurrection of Jesus Christ. Pray to God every day, asking for his help and deliverance.

Then, the power of God's love in Christ will light-up your life. The bright and clear light of God's love will shine upon you and fill your heart, and that is the greatest power of all.

No more power failures, just God's love. No more darkness, but only light. No more dead batteries, but only Christ. Amen!

NO MORE EXCUSES: Isaiah 25:6-9 & Matthew 22:1-14

Some people who had car accidents were asked to summarize on their insurance forms what had happened to them. The following are some true statements taken from people who had auto accidents.

- "Coming home, I drove into the wrong driveway and hit a tree I don't have."
- "I collided with a stationary truck coming the other way."
- "The guy was all over the road – I had to swerve a number of times before I hit him."
- "My car was legally parked when it backed into the other vehicle."
- "I had been driving my car for over 40 years and I fell asleep at the wheel and had an accident."
- "An invisible car came out of nowhere, stuck my vehicle and vanished."
- "The pedestrian had no idea of which way to go, so I ran over him."
- "The telephone pole was approaching fast - I was attempting to swerve out of its path when it struck me."
- "I was on my way to the doctor with rear end trouble when my universal joint gave way, causing me to have an accident."

- "I was backing out of a parking space and by the time I'd backed out far enough to see if anything was coming, it was already there."

- "I pulled away from the side of the road, glanced at my mother-in-law and headed over the embankment."

We all have our excuses. Today, we hear about how God invites us to his party, but everyone has their excuses why they cannot attend. In fact, Jesus tells a parable about a king who gave a wedding feast for his son.

The king sends out all of his servants to invite everyone he knows. But the people started giving their excuses about why they cannot come. "Not now, I'm too busy." "I've got other stuff to do."

Everybody has their excuses why they cannot attend the big party. Yet, the party is all set. Everything is ready and prepared. It is all ready to go, and you are invited!

You are invited to the big celebration the heavenly Father is giving in honor of his Son. That's right. The King invites you to the wedding banquet of his Son. The call goes out to everyone. "Invite to the wedding feast as many as you can find."

Everything is ready, and you are invited to the party – God's party. That is what heaven will be like – the greatest party the universe has ever seen. Heaven is a party, a celebration, a time of joy and laughter, music and singing.

Imagine having a life with no more pain or sorrow, no more sickness or disease, no more suffering or death. Imagine a world where there is no more bloodshed or acts of violence, no more war or terrorism. Imagine a life free from accidents or disasters, no more poverty, hunger or hardship.

Imagine not worrying all the time about your finances or your family. Imagine being completely happy and carefree. Imagine having perfect health and strength and vitality.

That is exactly what heaven will be like in God's new creation. This planet Earth and the entire universe will be regenerated and restored to God's original intentions. And we will experience a new and better life that we can barely describe or comprehend right now.

And the good news is that you are invited to the God's party. Everything has been prepared. We are all set and ready to go. You do not have to do anything. Just come as you are. God's grand party awaits you!

But strangely enough, we say, "No." We say, "Thanks, but no thanks." "My kids are playing sports." "I've got to catch up at work." "I have company coming over." "I've got to rake the leaves." "I've got a bunch of stuff I have to do." "Sorry, but I just don't have the time right now."

And so, we make our excuses. The things of God really don't interest us that much. The King and his Son can wait. We've got better things to do – or so we think.

Isn't that strange? When it comes to our everyday life, we always give it our best shot. No excuses here. We do everything necessary to improve our everyday existence. We eat right and exercise. We strive to improve our situation in life. We do lots of busy activities and run around all over the place. Our physical life is quite stimulating and active.

But what about our soul? What about our spiritual life? What about our faith and love for God? What about our eternal destiny? That somehow seems less important. We push all that spiritual stuff aside. Heaven can wait.

And so, we convince ourselves this temporal, earthly life is more important than eternity. We think we don't have time right now for God. We never pick up a Bible to read it. We don't pray. We don't attend worship. We neglect Holy Communion. Our spiritual life is dead and dormant. Our soul has shriveled up and died.

We live only for ourselves, and then, we wonder why everything seems to fall apart for us. We wonder why our life is in such disarray, why everything seems so hard, and why we are so unhappy and upset all the time. Maybe we should give God a chance.

Maybe we should listen to the Father as he calls us, as he invites us to come to himself. God wants to bestow his peace upon you. He wants you to have a rich and full life, a life filled with joy and peace, a life that will never end.

Everything has been prepared and made ready. A rich and vibrant spiritual life awaits you. The Lord is ready to bestow his grace upon you. It's all set. Everything is prepared. You can have something permanent and lasting, a life filled with endless possibilities and potential.

But here is the shocker. We still have our excuses. We continue to cling to our feeble reasons why we don't need God in our life. We continue to push the Lord away and say, "No thanks. I'm not interested." We reject the free gift God wants to give us.

Why does this happen? What is going on? Well, the basic problem here is that we are rebels. We instinctively turn away from the things of God. We resist God every chance we get. We have a pathological aversion to the words and promises of God.

And this stubborn attitude infects our entire system. It affects our body, mind and spirit. It totally messes up our thinking and logic. It affects our ability to reason and make sound decisions.

This rebellion started with the fall of Adam and Eve. That's when humanity went off the rails. That's when our spiritual malaise set in. We lost our spiritual health. We lost our sanity. We no longer can understand what is really important and what really matters in the end. We lost paradise and that perfect life we all yearn for. We lost God.

But that is precisely why the Son of the King comes into this world. Our Lord comes to rescue us from our rebellion. He comes to heal our spiritual sickness. He comes to restore our body, mind and spirit. He comes to change our thinking and ability to make the right decisions. He comes to bring us back to the source of all true life – God.

In the words of Isaiah the prophet, "On this mountain, the Lord will provide a rich feast, a lavish banquet for all people. God will swallow up death forever. He will wipe away the tears from all faces, for the Lord has spoken."

Isaiah is speaking of a day when death will be swallowed up forever. Our tears will be wiped away. Our hearts will be lifted up and changed. God will change us and recreate us in the image of his Son.

Isaiah declares that on God's holy mountain, something special will be provided for all people. On this mountain, God will set-up and establish a rich feast, a lavish banquet. On this mountain, God will give his Son to suffer and die for us.

This promised mountain is none other than Mount Calvary, a hill outside of the city of Jerusalem. There, the Son of the King was crucified. There, he took our spiritual sickness upon himself. He let our rebellion kill him. He gives himself for us.

The perfectly healthy Son becomes infected with our disease. He is contaminated with our fatal condition. Christ becomes the ultimate sinner. "God made him who had no sin, to be sin for us, so that in him, we might become the righteousness of God."

On this mountain, the Son of God was crucified. There, on Golgotha, the place of the skull, he bears our burden and suffers our punishment. "On the mount of the Lord, it will be provided." "This is love, not that we have loved God, but that he loved us, and sent his Son to be the atoning sacrifice for our sins."

Through this death on Mount Calvary, sins are forgiven and a healing fountain is opened. The blood of Christ now brings a cleansing of our soul and a healing for our spirit, mind and body.

In Christ, God himself restores to us eternal life and the gates of paradise are reopened. The Lord now breaks through all of our excuses. He restores our sanity and opens our eyes to see the truth right before us.

We now can truly perceive that God is calling to us in grace. We can hear, "On this mountain, God has provided a great and rich feast for everyone, a lavish banquet for all people. Death has been swallowed up forever. The Messiah has risen from the dead and the way to God's new creation is now wide open. Come and enter the kingdom of the Father!"

This is a Word that bestows life and forgiveness. A Word delivers what it says. God speaks and it comes to pass. The Word of God is powerful and creative.

This is exactly why we come to worship. "Faith comes from hearing the word, and the word is heard through the message of Christ." Jesus says, "If you hold to my teaching, you will be my disciples and the truth will set you free."

Here, at worship, the Lord speaks to our deepest needs. He sees our hurts and wounds, and he says, "Take heart! Your sins are forgiven. Be at peace; you are loved by God." He says, "Those who hope in the Lord will renew their strength. They will soar on wings like eagles; they will run and not grow weary." "Behold, this is our God; we have waited for him and he saved us. This is the Lord; we waited for him. Let us be glad and rejoice in his salvation."

At worship, we discover once again the healing power of Christ. We are spiritually refreshed. We come with all of our troubles and sorrows, all of hurts and pains, and all of our fears and worries. We bring our heavy burden once again to the mountain of the Lord and we lay it down at the foot of the cross.

There, on the cross of Golgotha, we see our Savior who gave himself for us. There, we receive that peace of God that passes all understanding. "On this mountain, the Lord will provide."

Today, we remember that we are safe in God's love. We have the promise of something special, something this world cannot offer. This is God's invitation to something brand new - a new beginning and a new life. This is that invitation to the greatest party in the universe, a party that is never going to end.

No more excuses. Let's not miss out on this celebration. The invitation has gone out to all people. The call has gone forth. Let's make sure we respond with faith. Let us take God's Word to heart, and continue to put our trust in Christ, our Savior.

"This is our God; we trusted in him and he saved us." "This is the Lord; let us rejoice and be glad and celebrate his salvation." No more excuses. Come on, the party is about to begin! Amen!

FORGETTING THE PAST: Philippians 3:1-14

Poor old Charlie Brown had just lost another baseball game. Lucy walks over to him, puts her hands on her hips, and says, "Charlie Brown, you are a foul ball in the game of life. You are a missed free throw, a shanked nine iron, a called third strike. You are a blocked punt, a dropped fly ball, a seven-ten split in the tenth frame. You are a missed field goal in overtime and three putts on the eighteenth green. Have I made myself clear?"

As she walks away, Linus comes over and says, "Don't feel bad, Charlie Brown. They say you learn more from your defeats than from your victories." Charlie Brown says, "If that's true, then I'm the smartest person in the world."

Do you ever feel like Charlie Brown? We may learn from our defeats, but it's hard. Our past mistakes have a way of repeating themselves. Our past defeats really bother us. We keep getting stuck in what happened to us long ago. Sometimes, the past can have a powerful hold on us.

Everyone has a past. Today, the Apostle Paul talks about his former life. Did you know that Paul was once a Pharisee and a very strict one at that? Paul was very proud to have been a Hebrew, from the tribe of Benjamin.

Paul says that he kept the Law of Moses blamelessly; he followed the Torah completely. Paul put his confidence in himself and in his obedience. He trusted in his own righteousness. He was a zealous Pharisee.

If anyone ever had the right to brag about his life, Paul did. He was totally committed to keeping the Law of Moses. However, later, he would admit that he was on the wrong track.

You see, Paul the Pharisee was a persecutor of the church. He hunted down Christians and arrested them. He even took part in the murder of Stephan, the first Christian martyr. Paul rejected Jesus - he thought he was a false Messiah. Therefore, he tried to destroy the church of God.

Yet, years later, Paul could say, "Forgetting what lies behind, I strain forward to what lies ahead. I press on toward the goal, to win the prize for which God has called me heavenward in Christ Jesus."

How is this possible? How can Paul say, "I forget what lies behind and I move forward?" How is it possible to stop thinking all the time about the past?

It's hard to forget the past, isn't it? The past has a way of coming back to us every day. It is constantly overshadowing our present reality. We cannot help but think back to the grief and loss we have experienced. We remember the mistakes we have made, all the stupid things we have done, all the foolish decisions we regret, all the failures and miscues we wish we could undo.

We remember all the bad things we have done, and it really bothers us. It makes us ashamed and sorry. We are filled with regret and remorse. We wrestle with a guilty conscience.

Years ago, a young man was arrested and convicted for burglary in New York City. How did the police catch him? As he began his burglary of a high-rise apartment, he noticed a statue of Jesus on the mantelpiece. He could not stand this figure of Jesus watching him, so he carefully turned it around, leaving fingerprints in the process.

Imagine the regret he must have felt, as he sat in his prison cell constantly replaying that mistake over and over again. We have a tendency to do the same thing. We sit in the prison cell of the past, constantly replaying all of our mistakes repeatedly.

How can we forget the past? How can we let it go and be set free? How can we move forward in our life?

When Paul talks about his former life, he confesses that he was on the wrong track. All that talk about being blameless and trusting in his own righteousness was a delusion. It is not possible to be blameless under God's Law. We can never be righteous enough when we stand before God. The problem here is that we are all sinners. That is why we constantly fall back in the same old sins again and again.

The truth is that we have a hard time obeying God's Law. We find it much easier to do what is wrong. Therefore, we have no righteousness when we stand before the Almighty God.

That is why Paul says, "Whatever gain I thought I had in my former life, I count as loss for the sake of Christ." Then, Paul says, "I want to know Christ, I want to gain Christ, I want to be found in him. Then, I will have a righteousness that is not my own, but the very righteousness of Christ, the righteousness that comes from God."

Paul tells us that Christ is our hope. He is our righteousness. Jesus Christ, the Son of God does what we are unable to do. He takes our defeats and turns them into victories.

Back when Paul was still persecuting Christians, he decided to expand his operation and travel to other cities. Paul was going up to Damascus to arrest the Christians there. He was on a "seek and destroy" mission. He was determined to stamp out Christianity once and for all.

Then, as Paul was traveling on the road to Damascus, a blinding flash of light knocked him to the ground, and a voice said, "Paul, Paul, why are you persecuting me?" Paul cried out, "Who are you?" "I am Jesus, the one you are persecuting. Now get up and go into the city and you will be told what to do."

Paul was then led by hand into Damascus. He had been blinded by the light and could not see. For three days, he sat in total darkness, thinking about what had just happened. Paul probably thought about his whole life and what a mistake he had made in persecuting Christians and trying to destroy the church of God.

Now he knew. Jesus was the true Messiah promised by God in the Old Testament. And he had risen from the dead. Christ was alive; it was just as his followers were proclaiming – Christ has risen! He has risen, indeed.

Now, Paul understood that this Jesus of Nazareth was more than just a carpenter from Galilee. He is the very Son of the Living God. Moreover, Paul learned that Christ could take a hardened sinner who is headed down the wrong track, and totally turn his life around.

That is grace. The Risen Lord steps into our life, and he completely changes us.

That's why Paul the Apostle will speak of Jesus so much. He is the Savior of the entire world. He is the Lord of Life and the King of Kings. He is the Lamb of God who takes away the sins of the world. He is the Bread of Life and the Living Water. He is the Crucified One who has risen from the dead. He is the Resurrection and the Life. He is that Light of the world that appeared to Paul on the road to Damascus.

Whenever we think about our past and all the mistakes we have made, we need to turn to Jesus Christ, the Son of God. He takes all of our defeats, mistakes and failures upon himself. He carries our sins to the cross. There, our Lord pays the price for us. He suffers our punishment. He dies our death. He pays the price for our past.

In this way, our past is taken away. God remembers our sins no more! The blood of Jesus Christ cleanses us from all sin.

Here is the key to forgetting the bad parts of your past – God's forgiveness in Christ. If God has forgiven you, then you can forgive yourself. You can forgive yourself for all the bad things you have done.

Forgive yourself, and forget all those things that bother you so. Don't let them control your present life. Let them go. Let the blood of Christ cleanse your conscience and soul.

Forget what lies behind, and move forward to what lies ahead. Press on towards the goal, the prize of that upward call of God in Christ Jesus. Don't live in defeat, but rejoice in God's victory in Jesus Christ. That is what Paul tells the Philippians, and that is what he is telling us today.

Paul says, "I press on, to take hold of that for which Christ Jesus took hold of me." "I strain toward what lies ahead." "I move forward, forgetting the past."

This doesn't mean that we just ignore the past, and pretend these things never happened. It means that we acknowledge and confess to God whatever may be bothering us about the past. We give to God our burden, and we say, "Here, Lord. I cannot handle this anymore by myself. I now give it all to you."

Like Paul the Apostle, we then find a gracious Savior who bestows forgiveness and grace. The Light of the world shines upon us and we see the glory of Christ revealed through his cross and resurrection. We discover, "By his wounds, we are healed."

Like Paul, we discover a righteousness that is not our own, a righteousness that comes from God. This is not something we are able to create or establish by our own efforts or works.

This righteousness of God is a free gift bestowed upon blind and lost sinners - it is pure grace. That's exactly what Paul the Pharisee discovered on the road to Damascus.

This is the righteousness of God's Messiah - it is the perfect life of Christ that now totally covers all of your life. It covers the past, the present and the future. Your entire life is now covered by the perfect obedience of Jesus. He kept the Law of Moses on our behalf.

Jesus of Nazareth fully and completely obeyed the Torah. He did what even the best Pharisee could never do. He perfectly fulfilled all the requirements of God's Law.

In other words, God now reckons the perfect obedience of Christ to you. You are covered with the Messiah's righteousness. It is as if you have kept the Law perfectly and completely.

Now, you are set free to love God and to serve him with real joy and true gladness. Now, you can embrace a future that is rich in possibility. "Forgetting what is behind and straining toward what is ahead, I press on towards the goal."

Through Jesus, we can forget what lies behind us. We can realize that the past is gone; we can let it go. Now, we can live each day knowing that our sins are forgiven. We are justified by grace, through faith in Christ as our Savior. God declares us righteous.

Listen, you are loved by a gracious God, and he wants to fill your life with peace and purpose. Therefore, look to the future with confidence and hope. Press on towards the goal of God's new creation.

Keep on living by faith. Focus on Christ and celebrate his gifts of grace. Follow the upward call of God. Follow the Way, the Truth and the Life. Forget the past and embrace your future. Upward and onwards! Amen!

134

YOU HAVE TREASURE IN HEAVEN: Mark 10:17-31

The story is told of a bishop in the Church of England, who long ago delivered a rousing sermon. He talked about how our earthly possessions do not last forever. This present life is temporary. We are not here forever.

The bishop said our greatest treasure is the gift of eternal life that God freely gives to lost sinners. That is our treasure in heaven and it will last forever. However, in this life, our possessions will eventually fade away. They are temporary, at best. In fact, we do not really own anything in this life. Everything really belongs to God.

A wealthy parishioner was greatly offended by the bishop's sermon, and he told him so after the service. In fact, later that week, the rich man invited the bishop over to his estate for lunch. After lunch, he took the bishop on an extended tour of his property. He showed him his huge mansion, his elaborate gardens, his beautiful woodlands and his elegant stable.

When the tour was over, the rich man finally said, "Now then, are you still going to tell me that all these buildings and land really don't belong to me." The bishop smiled, and said,

"Ask me that same question a hundred years from now."

Today we hear about the story of a rich man who encounters Jesus. Our Lord is on his way to Jerusalem. A large crowd is following him. Suddenly, a man runs up to Jesus and falls on his knees before him.

He cries out, "Good teacher - would must I do to inherit eternal life?" And Jesus says, "Why do you call me good? No one is good except God alone. You know the commandments: Do not murder, do not commit adultery, do not steal, do not bear false testimony, do not defraud, honor your father and mother."

And the man said to him, "Teacher, all these commandments I have kept from my youth. Surely, there must be something more." And Mark says, "Jesus looked at the man and loved him."

Jesus loved him, even though he was dead wrong. This guy really thought he was keeping all the commandments of God, but he was wrong. We do not keep the commandments the way God wants us to. We do not fully and perfectly obey the law of God. We do not always put God first in our life, and it shows in the way we live and think.

We may deceive ourselves and say, "I'm not really that bad. I try to do what's right. I'm basically a good person." But Jesus says point blank - "No one is good. No one is good, except God alone."

The truth is we all fall short of the perfect obedience and love God is looking for. In the Sermon on the Mount, Jesus takes the commandments and applies them to our hearts.

He shows us how the commandments of God deal not just with our external actions, but also with our inner attitude and thoughts. The law reveals what is really inside our hearts.

For example, Jesus will say that the commandment, "Do not murder," means we should not hurt or harm anyone. Our Lord will say that if you hate anyone, then it is the same as if you have committed murder in God's eyes.

In the same way, Jesus says that if you look at someone with lust in your heart, then, in God's eyes, you have committed adultery.

Again, if you think about cheating on your income taxes, you are stealing. Or if you are spreading malicious gossip, you are giving false testimony. If you neglect your parents, you are not honoring your father and mother.

If you are not honest in your dealings with others, you are committing fraud.

You see, the law of God reveals what is inside our hearts. It judges our thoughts and attitudes. It shows us our true condition. We are sinners, and we have a real problem with hatred and lust, greed and envy, selfishness and pride.

No one is good, except God alone. We all fall short in some way. All of us have a different weakness, a different area in our life where we continually fail.

For one person, it might be the love of money; for another, it might be alcohol or drugs. For some, it's a self-righteous attitude; for others, it's jealousy or envy. For someone else, it might be a constant lying and a basic untruthfulness. For some, it's fighting, arguing, and making trouble. For others, it's a lack of faith and doubt in God's Word. We could go on.

We all have our weak spots. And that's why the commandments come to us, and they speak a word of judgment. They are like a mirror that shows our true reflection. They reveal our true condition when we stand before God.

Therefore, Jesus uses the commandments to show this rich man his sore spot. He wants him to see that he wasn't truly keeping the law of God.

Jesus says to him, "Okay, so you keep all the commandments, do you? Okay, but you still lack one thing - go and sell everything you have, and give that money to the poor. Then, you will have treasure in heaven, and you will be able to follow me."

Our Lord says, "Take all of your money and throw it away!" And the man says, "What do you mean, 'Throw it away?' I can't do that! I've worked hard to get everything I have. I'm not just going to throw it all away. I've given my whole life over to accumulating all my possessions."

"Exactly!" says Jesus. "That's just it. You've given your whole life over to money and possessions. You worship your possessions more than you worship God. You need to stop serving those things, and seek first the kingdom of God."

Christ says, "No one can serve two masters. Either he will hate the one and love the other, or he will be devoted to the one and despise the other. You cannot serve both God and money."

You see, our Lord wanted this man to realize that he wasn't keeping the first commandment, much less the rest of them.

Jesus knew his spiritual condition. He knew that he was not putting God first in his life. Therefore, Christ tells him to give away his earthly possessions.

Remember, Christ looked at this man and loved him. He loved him! Moreover, he wanted him to see that salvation is totally a free gift of God. There is nothing we can do to merit eternal life. Salvation is a gift. We are saved by grace alone.

No one is good except God alone. No one is good enough to go to heaven. We are all lost sinners, and we are all trapped by our earthly desires and constant shortcomings.

But the good news today is that Christ has come to seek out and save lost sinners like you and me. The Lord looks at our situation and he loves us. He loves us, even though he knows we are dead wrong.

In fact, the Son of Gods loves us so much that he came down from heaven and fully enters our life. He humbles himself and he becomes like us. The Son becomes incarnate. He takes on our own flesh and blood, and he lives our life in this fallen world.

"When the time had fully come, God sent his Son to be born of a woman, born under the Law of God, to redeem those under the Law of God."

The Son of God becomes like us in every single way – every way, but one. Christ was without sin. He was perfect. He never committed any sin or broke any of the commandments. He kept the law perfectly in thought, word and deed. None of us are good, except Christ alone.

In this way, our Lord does everything necessary so that we might inherit eternal life. Jesus fulfills the law so that we might be made right with God. He obeys where we fail.

God the Father now covers our broken life with the life of Jesus. He covers up all of our imperfections with the perfection of Jesus. For the sake of Christ, God declares that you are now righteous, holy, and forgiven. You are a saint!

Imagine that! You are forgiven and made right with God. You have eternal life and are a now part of God's kingdom. In addition, you are now freed up to look at your life in a very different way. You can take your old life and your old way of thinking, and just throw them away!

Something different has come, and that something is the new and better life we have in Christ. This changes everything! It changes how we view our present earthly life, and how we think about the future that is to come. Now, our eyes are opened to see the powerful reality God presents to us in his Word.

I mean, think back to the question the bishop asked at the beginning of this sermon. Think about this: "Where will you be in a hundred years from now?"

Where will you be in a hundred years? Think about that.

The Bible teaches that for those who trust in Christ as their Lord and Savior, a new and better life exists. This is the life that we will experience after we die.

Remember, all of us will experience an earthly death. Our present life is temporary, at best. But there is another life to come after we die, one that is better and everlasting.

And that new life in Christ is what we will be experiencing one hundred years from now, in God's new creation. As the creed confesses, "I believe in the resurrection and the life of the world to come."

And when you truly comprehend this reality, it totally changes the way you view your present life. It helps you deal with the problems we all experience and the burdens we all carry. You can now take your old limited way of thinking and just throw it away.

For example, when it comes to money and finances, you do not have to live in constant anxiety. You don't have to worry so much about your life and how you are going to pay the bills. You do not have to be fearful of the future.

Remember, your earthly possessions are temporary, at best. If you try to rely on them to make you happy and content, you are going to be disappointed. Material things can only take you so far. Everything has an expiration date.

Don't get me wrong; in this life, we may enjoy many material blessings. You may have lots of money and possessions, and there is nothing wrong with that.

There are many rich people in the Bible who are great examples of faith, hope and perseverance. However, their possessions never got in the way of believing in God's promises.

For example, Abraham and Sarah were very wealthy. So was Joseph, in the end. Job and King David were also rich. Nicodemus and Joseph of Arimathea are other examples.

But all of these saints knew that there is more to life than just having wealth and money. They didn't worry all the time about their finances and how they were going to make it. They knew there is more to life than just having earthly possessions. They knew they had treasure in heaven, and the same is true for us.

You have treasure in heaven! You have Christ. You have eternal life. You have the gift of salvation. You are a saint, a child of God who is deeply loved by the heavenly Father.

That is why you can let go of your worries, fears, and burdens. Lay them down at the foot of the cross. Receive that peace which only Christ can give.

Jesus says, "Do not worry so much about your life. Who by worrying can add a single hour to his earthly life? But seek first God's kingdom and the righteous he gives, and your Father in heaven will take care of you. He knows what you need. God will provide."

Our Lord says, "Do not worry about tomorrow, for tomorrow can worry about itself. Each day has enough trouble of its own. Nevertheless, seek to serve God and love him only. Put God first in your life. And then, come and follow me, and you will have treasure in heaven."

You have treasure in heaven! You have Jesus Christ, the Son of God. You have the gifts he freely gives, the gifts of God's love, forgiveness, and a new and better life to come. This is your treasure in heaven, and it will last one hundred years, a thousand years, a million years and more. It will last forever!

Therefore, be at peace. Remember that God loves you, and Christ is with you now and each day to come, forevermore. Amen!

THE LORD NEEDS IT: Luke 19:28-48

The account of our Lord's entry into Jerusalem on Palm Sunday is familiar to most of us. We have heard this story before. However, there are many great lessons here for us today.

When we look at our text again, we first see how the Lord is in control of the situation. The Lord is in control, even as he goes to the cross. Jesus knew exactly what would soon happen to him, and he goes willingly and obediently.

We note that Palm Sunday was no accident. Christ wanted to make a public statement as he enters Jerusalem for the last time. He will enter as the Messiah King who fulfills all of God's promises in the Old Testament. "Rejoice greatly, O daughter of Zion! Shout, daughter of Jerusalem! See, your king comes to you, righteous and having salvation, gentle and riding on a donkey, on a colt, the foal of a donkey. He will proclaim peace to the nations. His rule will extend to the ends of the earth."

Luke tells us that before Jesus entered Jerusalem, he sent two of his disciples ahead of him, saying to them, "Go to the village ahead of you, and as you enter it, you will find a colt tied there, which no one has ever ridden. Untie it and bring it here. If anyone asks you, 'Why are you untying it?' tell them, 'The Lord needs it.'"

Now try to put yourself into the place of these two disciples. It is as if Jesus were telling you, "I want to go down to the Stop & Shop parking lot. There, you will find an unlocked BMW with the keys in the ignition. Get in the car and bring it to me. If anyone asks you what you are doing, just tell them the Lord needs it."

What do you think those two disciples were saying to each other as they walked into that village? Did they say something like, "Hey, I'm not too sure this is a good idea." "I'm not going to untie this donkey. You can grab it while I keep a lookout." "Perhaps we should turn back and forget the whole thing."

It is interesting that the two disciples didn't turn back or start quibbling. They didn't stand there and debate the issue. There's an important lesson here for us. These disciples trusted the Lord's plan. They knew that if Christ says something, that's good enough. We shouldn't question God's Word or start doubting his purpose for our life. We should always trust the Lord and believe his Word.

Those two disciples were sent ahead went and they found it was just as Christ had told them. It was exactly as he told them. In addition, as they were untying the colt, its owners did ask them, "Why are you untying our donkey?" And so, they replied, "The Lord needs it."

Now imagine you are the owners of this colt. You are sitting there and suddenly two scruffy looking characters come up to your favorite donkey. They start untying it to lead it away. You say, "Hey, what are you doing there? Why are you untying my colt?" "The Lord needs it." "Oh, I see. Okay, if the Lord needs it, go right ahead." With an understanding nod of the head, the owners release the donkey immediately to the two disciples.

"The Lord needs it." End of discussion. Notice that the owners loaned out their donkey because they saw Jesus as their Lord. When they heard that, "The Lord Jesus needs it," the discussion was over. They didn't start up with a bunch of questions like, "How long do you need my donkey? How far will you travel? Will you bring him back when you are finished? Will you sign this rental agreement? Can you give us a deposit before you leave?" If the Lord needs it, that settles it. End of discussion.

I think the owners of the donkey really demonstrated their faith, and it was a specific faith in the Lord Jesus Christ. They knew that Christ was in their area. They knew what Jesus had been doing in his ministry.

Do not forget that only a few weeks earlier, Jesus had raised Lazarus from the dead in Bethany, the village right next door. Many people in Jerusalem knew about that miracle. In fact, some were even present at the cemetery and were eyewitnesses of what happened. They saw what happened when Jesus cried out, "Lazarus, come forth!" Therefore, lots of people knew that Jesus and his disciples were in the area and were about to enter Jerusalem for the Passover.

That's lesson number three. Faith is always specific. Our faith is in the Lord Jesus Christ, the Messiah King revealed to us in the Bible. We don't follow some imaginary character from mythology. This isn't a make-believe story about fables and tall tales. This Jesus of Nazareth really walked on this planet over 2,000 years ago. He really went about preaching and teaching and healing the sick. He worked incredible miracles; he even raised the dead. Thousands of people were eyewitnesses of these miracles. They saw what he did, they heard what he said and they followed him wherever he went.

Moreover, many of these eyewitnesses report to us in the New Testament exactly what they saw and heard. They testify that this carpenter from Galilee is the Son of God. He really was born of the virgin Mary. He did actually die on the cross for our sins. He literally rose from the dead on Easter morning. They saw Jesus after the resurrection. They even touched him and confirmed that he really rose from the dead.

This Jesus of Nazareth really did enter Jerusalem on the back of a donkey that was borrowed from someone else. As Luke tells us, "The people spread their cloaks on the ground and they waved their palm branches. The whole crowd of disciples then began joyfully to praise God in loud voices for all the miracles they had seen." (Note again that phrase, "all the miracles they had seen." These people were eyewitnesses to what Christ was doing.)

There is one more important lesson that Palm Sunday teaches us. There were two groups of people on that momentous day. There were the disciples who joyfully praised God and sang, "Blessed is the king who comes in the name of the Lord! Peace in heaven and glory in the highest!" These disciples were simple folk, but they knew that there was something very special about this carpenter from Galilee and so they followed him. They believed in him and trusted his Word.

Then there were the Pharisees who were also in the crowd that day. They actually complained about what the disciples were doing. They stood on the sidelines and started complaining to Jesus. They said, "Teacher, rebuke your disciples!" And Jesus replied, "If they keep quiet, even the stones will cry out."

In other words, this second group knew all about Jesus and what he was doing. They also knew all about the miracles and the raising of Lazarus, but they did not believe in the Messiah King. They rejected his claim upon their life – they refused to believe his Word. They lacked faith.

So, which group are you in? The issue today is the same as it was on that first Palm Sunday. Today, Jesus declares himself to be the true King sent by God. He comes to redeem and save lost sinners. He comes to go to the cross and to suffer the passion. The declaration is the same - and so is the choice. Will you acknowledge him as your King, or will you simply stand on the sidelines and complain?

In the end, it is not really about someone's donkey, but it is about your heart. By the grace of God and by the power of the Holy Spirit, we are those who trust in Jesus Christ as our Lord and Savior. He is the Lord of our life. He is our Savior. He is in control of everything that happens. He is the King who humbles himself and becomes our servant. He wears a crown of thorns as dies on the cross for our sins. Then, the Father exalts him through his glorious resurrection.

Christ is our King and we follow him in faith. What he commands, we will do. Where he sends us, we will go. What he asks for, we will gladly give. If the Lord needs it, we gladly obey. We now give of ourselves in love and service to others.

Listen. The Lord needs for you to be his witness and his servant. You are now called to put your faith into practice and to love and serve others. Go and tell others that the Messiah King has come. Share the gift you have received. Testify that this man from Galilee is the true of Son of God. He is the promised Savior.

As we do this together, we sing our praises to our Messiah King We celebrate and give thanks. We sing, "Hosanna in the highest! Blessed is he who comes in the name of the Lord. Hosanna in the highest! Thanks be to God for the gift of his Son! Blessed is the King who comes in the name of the Lord!" Amen!

THE WATER OF LIFE: John 4:5-26

The story is told of a young couple who were getting married. They planned a big wedding reception with lots of people. The bride asked the cake decorator to inscribe a special Bible verse on top of the cake. She wanted 1 John 4:18, which reads, "There is no fear in love, but perfect love casts out fear." Unfortunately, the cake decorator didn't know the Bible very well.

Now, the bride and groom did not see the cake until it was wheeled into the reception hall in front of all the guests. Imagine their surprise when they looked down and saw, not 1 John 4:18, but John 4:18, which reads, "You have had five husbands and the man you have now is not your husband." Surprise!

Today we see another surprise. We see how Jesus meets a Samaritan woman. You know how the Jews felt about the Samaritans. They considered them a cult. They were religious heretics because the Samaritans mixed their worship of God with various pagan rituals. That is why a Jew would never approach or talk to a Samaritan. They just did not associate together.

John tells us that Jesus and his disciples were traveling through the region of Samaria. They came to a town called Sychar. Jacob's well was there and Jesus was tired, so he sat down beside the well. It was about noon. The sun was bright and hot. The disciples had gone into town to buy some food.

That was when a Samaritan woman came to the well to draw some water. That was a bit unusual. Most people went to the well very early in the morning when it was still cool. No one came at noon to draw water. That was "siesta time," the hottest time of the day.

In fact, the drawing of water in the morning was a time of great socializing. Everyone would go down to the community well, get water and catch up on the latest news.

But not this woman. She comes at noon so that she could avoid contact with other people. Apparently, she was a social outcast, a loner. Yet, Jesus asked her for a drink. "I thirst," he said to her. "Can you give me a drink?"

The woman is shocked. "How is it that you, a Jew, are asking me for a drink?" Jesus answered her, "If you knew the gift of God and who it is that asks you for a drink, you would have asked him and he would have given you living water."

The woman then said, "Sir, you have no bucket and the well is deep. Where can you get that living water?" Jesus said, "Everyone who drinks of this water will be thirsty again. But whoever drinks of the water that I give will never be thirsty. The water that I give will become in them a spring of water gushing up to eternal life."

This catches the woman's attention. She says, "Sir, give me this water." And Jesus says, "Go, call your husband and come back." The woman answers, "I have no husband." "You are right in saying, 'I have no husband,' for you have had five husbands and the man you have now is not your husband."

Notice how Jesus knew all about this woman and her situation in life. She had made a mess of things, and most people probably thought she was a lost cause. They looked down on her and she wanted to avoid their condemnation.

Yet, Jesus still reaches out to her. He knew all about her life and he still loved her. And so it is for us. We are no different from this woman.

We may not be Samaritans, but we are sinners, people who have fallen away from God. We struggle to obey God's Word, and we also have our past. We have those things in our life we are ashamed of. We have skeletons in our closet, too.

We are no different from this Samaritan woman. We also have our guilt and regrets. Our past bothers us. However, the Lord did not give-up on this woman and he doesn't give-up on us either.

It was noontime when this woman came to the well. Jesus said to her, "I am thirsty. Can you give me a drink?"

Now, let me take you to another place. It would be noontime on another day. The place is another city, Jerusalem. Outside this city, a man hangs on a cross. He suffers great pain and agony. At the end of his suffering, he cries out, "I thirst!"

He who had the water of life was dying of thirst. He who had the living water was parched. He who bestows eternal life was dying on a cross. Here we see how the Son of God cries out for a drink.

He is dying of thirst as he carries our sins and our past. He carries all of our guilt and regrets. He bears our burden and dies our death. He takes all of sins down into the depths of hell where they belong. "I thirst!"

Our Lord dies on that cross so that we would never go thirsty. He dies so that we might receive life. That is the good news today. Through our Lord's death on the cross we do receive the water of life. Sins are forgiven and our thirst is quenched. Christ is that Rock of Ages that was "cleft for me." The water of life gushes forth from his wounds.

God demonstrated his love for us in this: While we were still sinners, Christ died for us. Now, we have peace with God through our Lord Jesus Christ. We have peace and joy. A new day dawns! As St. Paul says, "God's love has been poured into our hearts through the Holy Spirit who has been given to us."

And, in the end, that is what God's grace is all about. You may think that you have made a mess of your life. You may think that God can never forgive you for what you have done. You may think that all is lost.

However, just like the Samaritan woman, no one is lost when they stand before Jesus. That woman received the grace of God. She asked for the living water and she abundantly drank from the water of life.

She drank and was satisfied. She was thirsty and was refreshed. God's love was poured out into her heart and things would never be the same for her.

And so it is for us. No one is beyond hope when they stand before the Lord Jesus. He is the Savior of the world. He endured all things for us so that he might freely bestow the gift of

God. He became thirsty so that we might drink freely. He died our death so that we might live.

Jesus says, "Whoever drinks of the water that I give will never be thirsty. The water I give will become a spring of water welling up to eternal life." Therefore, drink deeply of God's grace. Receive Christ as your Savior. Rejoice that your thirst has been quenched. And tell others that there is hope. There is Jesus. And he freely gives the water of life to all who need a new life and a second chance. Amen!

Here is a bonus sermon from the book,
No More Tears

NO MORE TEARS: John 11:17-44

I remember when I was a little kid I hated getting my hair washed. I knew that the shampoo would burn my eyes. That was such a painful experience. I would have to keep my eyes squeezed shut to prevent any of the shampoo from getting in.

Then my mother discovered something called "No More Tears" shampoo. This was is a much gentler shampoo with less irritating ingredients. It was specifically designed with children in mind. No More Tears! Thanks be to God!

Scientific studies indicate that crying is actually good for you. It helps to release emotional tension. Crying relaxes you. It calms you down.

However, while crying may be beneficial for us, the circumstances that trigger it are not. That is why tears usually symbolize tragedy and suffering. We consider crying something to be avoided.

However, all of us shed tears at some point in our life. No matter who we are, all of us cry. Some may be more private than others. We may choose to not let other people see us crying, but we all shed tears. When was the last time you cried?

When was the last time you really cried tears of anguish? Perhaps it was the death of someone special. The pain was simply too great for you to bear. Perhaps it was because of some marriage or family problem. Maybe your heart was broken by someone very close to you. Perhaps you saw a news report of a tragedy or some terrorist attack.

So many things can bring us grief. It can be the loss of a job or having to move. It can be financial troubles or an unsatisfying life. It can be the loneliness we experience. It can be the regret and remorse we feel over the stupid mistakes we have made in our life. It can be almost anything that brings us pain.

Wouldn't it be great if we lived in a world where tears would no longer be necessary? Wouldn't it be great if there were no more pain or sadness or grief?

What if we could live in a world where there is no more death or mourning or crying or pain? As we address these questions, let us look at the story of Lazarus in John 11.

First of all, we see how the Son of God knows all about our tears. We see how a close friend of Jesus has died. The Gospel of John tells us specifically that Jesus loved Lazarus and his two sisters, Martha and Mary. They were all close friends.

But now, Lazarus is dead. Jewish burial customs required that the body be buried on the day of death. The body was washed, anointed with perfume and spices, and wrapped in strips of linen. Then, the body was laid in a grave or a tomb.

So, Lazarus has died. He has been buried. The funeral has been held. Jesus now goes to visit his friends in Bethany. But notice how he is late for Lazarus' funeral. And he wasn't just a few minutes late, or even a few hours late, but he was a few days late.

It looks like Martha and Mary are hurt because Jesus was not there. They thought he could have healed their brother and prevented his death from even occurring. But now, it's too late.

The one they loved so dearly has been taken away from them. Lazarus is gone. This is undoubtedly why Martha and Mary are so upset with Jesus. Why didn't he come earlier when they called him? He could have prevented all this! However, he did not arrive until days later. Why?

We often are like Martha and Mary when we experience tragedy. We also have our questions. We also ask, "Why, Lord? Why did this have to happen? Why didn't you do something to prevent all this from occurring?"

We all have our questions. Martha even says to Jesus, "Lord, if you had been here, my brother would not have died." Mary says the same thing, too.

The Lord answers all of our questions with one of the greatest statements in the entire Bible. Jesus says to Martha, "I am the resurrection and the life. Whoever believes in me shall live, even though he dies. In fact, everyone believes in me shall never die. Martha, do you believe this?"

The Lord calls for us to believe in him, to believe even in the face of tragedy. We need to believe in Christ, even in the presence of death. We need to believe, even as we stand at the gravesite of a loved one.

Jesus is the resurrection and the life. Whoever believes in him shall live forever. Even though we pass through death, we shall live with him forever in a new and better life. Do you believe this?

And let's not think that our Lord stands aloof from our pain and tears. He doesn't simply look down upon us from high above and speak pious platitudes like, "Don't worry. You'll get over it. It will be all right. Time heals all. Just move on, and you'll be fine."

No, the Son of God fully enters into our pain and sorrow. Jesus is deeply troubled by this tragedy. He is deeply moved in spirit. He is always touched by our tragedy and grief. The Lord shares our sorrow. He cries our tears.

We now see how Christ goes to the tomb of his friend, Lazarus. He sees the sisters weeping in sorrow. He sees the anguish and heartache of the people gathered there. And Jesus himself weeps. He cries tears of sadness.

The Son of God fully enters into our suffering and pain. He cries our tears, and these tears remind us we never suffer alone. In Christ, God himself enters into our heartache and grief. God cries our tears.

Jesus not only weeps, but he also does something about our painful situation. He tells the sisters, "Roll away the stone." And so, they open the tomb by removing the stone that sealed it.

Then, Jesus cried out in a loud voice, "Lazarus, come forth!" And the man who had been dead for four days came out, his hands and feet covered with linen strips, and his face wrapped with a cloth. Jesus then said to them, "Unbind him and let him go!"

Here Christ demonstrates that he truly is the resurrection and the life. He is the Savior who gives life to the dead. He gives salvation to the lost and hope to the hopeless. Moreover, he does this by fully entering into our life and our death. The sinless Son of God will die on the cross for all of our sins.

And as Christ hangs upon that cross, the women who had followed from Galilee will watch him die. They will weep their tears of sadness. They will watch their Lord suffer and finally breathe his last.

Then, they will take his bruised and battered body down from the cross and will wrap it in strips of linen. A cloth will cover his face, just like the cloth that covered the face of Lazarus.

Jesus will then be quickly placed in a tomb. There will not be time on Good Friday to properly anoint his body with perfume and spices. The women will come back on Sunday morning to finish that job.

However, when they arrive at the tomb on Sunday morning, they discover that the tomb is empty. Only the strips of linen are lying there. Christ had risen from the dead, alive and victorious.

This proves that Jesus truly is the resurrection and the life. And when we put our faith in him, we discover that we are now able to cope with tragedy and heartache.

The resurrection of Christ changes everything. It fully redeems our suffering. We now discover that we can make it through those difficult times of our life. His resurrection gives us the power to keep going. His life gives us a new hope and his love reminds us that we are never alone.

The Son of God has truly entered into our world and into our life. He has cried our tears. He has died our death. He gave himself so that we might live forever. This is the victory that is yours right now, by faith. On the last day, you will fully and completely enter into it, for all time and eternity. On the last day, you will enter God's new creation.

Let's not forget the tremendous power of faith. When Job was in the midst of experiencing great suffering and pain, he looked to his Redeemer. Even after Job lost his family, his health, and his possessions, he could still confess, "I know that my Redeemer lives. I know that even though I die, I shall see him for myself. With my own eyes, I will behold him."

Job's faith was able to sustain him through the darkest hours of his life. Job was able to look forward to the last day and the victory that we will one day enter into. This is the victory of having our bodies raised from the dead and glorified.

It is the victory of seeing God face-to-face and living in his presence forevermore. It is the victory of being reunited with our loved ones who have gone before us. The Bible tells us that on that last day, there will be no more tears.

Now that is an amazing statement! From the time of Adam and Eve, tears have been shed over death, pain, sickness, tragedy, and endless disasters. How many oceans would all those tears fill? However, according to Revelation, a time is coming when there will be no more tears.

Revelation says, "On the last day, God will wipe the tears from our eyes, and there will be no more death or mourning or crying or pain. For the old order of things will have passed away. God will make all things new."

On that last day, God will renew this entire universe. In this renewed creation, we will have that perfect and complete life God intended for Adam and Eve to have in the first place. Then, there will be no more crying or pain. Then, God will wipe all our tears away forever.

No more tears! Do you remember what Jesus said to Martha? "I am the resurrection and the life. Whoever believes in me shall live forever. Martha, do you believe this?"

Do you believe this? Do you truly believe that Jesus is the resurrection and the life? Do you believe that death does not have the last word? Do you believe the victory is yours?

The day is coming when we will live together with Christ forever, and we shall see our loved ones again. With our own eyes, we shall behold our Redeemer and all the saints who have gone before us.

Such a hope can give us strength and courage. Such a faith is a powerful thing! It fills us with hope and the confidence that better days are coming.

Here is the bottom line to all of this: In this earthly life, we will all experience tears. We all experience pain and grief. We will experience the loss of our loved ones. And Jesus himself knew what it was like to go through all these things. The Lord understands our suffering.

But today our Lord promises us a new creation where tears of sorrow will never be shed again. No more tears! Here is a powerful hope that can help you to live with confidence and joy. You are safe in God's love. Jesus is your resurrection and life. Do you believe this? Amen!

Here is a bonus Bible Study from the book, "At the King's Table: Studies in Luke's Gospel"

LUKE 21:5-19: SIGNS OF THE END (I)

⁵As some spoke of the temple, how it was adorned with goodly stones and gifts, Jesus said,

⁶As for these things that ye behold, the days will come, in which there shall not be left one stone upon another that shall not be thrown down.

⁷They asked him, saying, Master, but when shall these things be? And what sign will there be when these things shall happen?

⁸He said, Take heed that ye be not deceived: for many shall come in my name, saying, I am Christ, and the time draweth near. Go ye not therefore after them.

⁹But when ye shall hear of wars and commotions, be not terrified: for these things must first come to pass, but the end is not by and by.

¹⁰Then he said unto them, Nation shall rise against nation, and kingdom against kingdom.

¹¹Great earthquakes shall be in divers places, and famines and pestilences, and fearful sights and great signs shall there be from heaven.

¹²But before all these, they shall lay their hands on you, and persecute you, delivering you up to the synagogues, and into prisons, being brought before kings and rulers for my name's sake.

¹³And it shall turn to you for a testimony.

¹⁴Settle it therefore in your hearts, not to meditate before what ye shall answer.

¹⁵For I will give you a mouth and wisdom, which all your adversaries shall not be able to gainsay nor resist.

¹⁶You shall be betrayed both by parents, and brethren, and kinsfolk, and friends; and some of you shall they cause to be put to death.

¹⁷And ye shall be hated of all men for my name's sake.

¹⁸But there shall not a hair of your head perish.

¹⁹In your patience, possess ye your souls.

Not One Stone upon Another

Our Lord Jesus plainly taught about the end of the world and his second coming. We now have a long section from Luke that looks at this. (We will divide this into four sections.) The fact that Jesus spent a lot of time teaching about this, shows how important it is.

This can be a confusing area for many people. It is certainly easy to overlook the main message, which our Lord is trying to communicate to us. We need to be careful not to get off track.

The first thing we need to notice is how the upcoming destruction of Jerusalem and the end of the world are woven together by Jesus. This long discourse comes in response to specific questions the disciples ask about the eventual destruction of the temple.

Luke tells us that the disciples remarked upon the beauty and magnificence of the temple in Jerusalem. This probably happened in the afternoon, as Jesus and his disciples were leaving the city. The sunlight shining upon the white marble and gold decorations that adorned the temple structure would have been a beautiful sight.

However, when the disciples remarked about the grandness of the temple, Jesus warned them that one day it would all be gone.

"As some spoke of the temple, how it was adorned with goodly stones and gifts, Jesus said, As for these things which ye behold, the days will come, in the which there shall not be left one stone upon another, that shall not be thrown down."

"And they asked him, saying, Master, but when shall these things be? And what sign will there be when these things shall come to pass?"

When Shall These Things Be?

Notice how the disciples ask when this would happen, and what will be signs that this is about to occur. The answer that Christ gives covers both the time before the destruction of Jerusalem by the Romans in A.D. 70 and the time before the end of the world. There will be clear and definitive signs that "these things shall come to pass."

A note about the Jewish-Roman War (A.D. 66-73): This was the first and largest of several uprisings against Roman rule in the land of Israel. The result was the destruction of numerous towns, the death and displacement of many people, and the complete destruction of the temple and the city of Jerusalem.

The revolt began in A.D. 66 with anti-taxation riots and terrorist attacks upon Roman citizens. The harsh reprisals by the Roman quickly escalated into all-out conflict. The Jewish forces had early success against the Roman armies, but the Emperor Nero would then dispatch his best generals, Vespasian and Titus, who assembled a massive military force and methodically marched down from Syria, destroying and subduing all opposition.

The first sign Jesus gives is that there will be numerous false prophets who will deceive many people. Some will even pretend to be the Messiah or a Savior sent from God. (This happened during the first Jewish-Roman War, and it continues even to this day.)

The next sign describes "war and commotion." Jesus says, "Nation shall rise against nation, and kingdom against kingdom." This is military conflict and armed warfare. It existed back then, and continues to exist even to this present day.

Jesus says, "Be not terrified: for these things must first come to pass; but the end is not by and by." Here is an important clue about how to understand these signs.

The nature of these signs is that they serve as a wake-up call. They are meant to remind us that now is the time to have faith. We need to be always prepared for the end (which could occur at any time) and watchful for our Lord's second coming. We have the certainty of ultimate triumph through Christ. Through his help, we are able to face the dark days ahead.

Jesus says, "So likewise ye, when ye see these things come to pass, knew ye that the kingdom of God is nigh at hand." "And when these things begin to come to pass, then look up, and lift up your heads; for your redemption draweth nigh."

Remember that Jesus was speaking to his original disciples. However, he is also speaking to us. That is the nature of these signs: They have been around since the day of the apostles, and they will continue to be around until the end. Again, the purpose of these signs is to remind us that the present is the time to believe. Today, we need to hold fast to what we confess.

In Divers Places

Christ now says, "And great earthquakes shall be in divers places, and famines, and pestilences; and fearful sights and great signs shall there be from heaven."

These "great signs from heaven" shall be large-scale natural disasters (hurricanes, typhoons, tsunamis, flooding, drought, volcanoes) as well as earthquakes and other seismic events. Included here also are pandemics and plagues, sickness and food shortages. (Again, notice how all of these things were common in the days of the Roman Empire, and they are still evident today.)

Ye Shall Be Hated

Christ then tells us how his followers may experience hatred, betrayal, family conflict, persecution, arrest and even execution. "And ye shall be hated of all men for my name's sake."

"But before all these, they shall lay their hands on you, and persecute you, delivering you up to the synagogues, and into prisons, being brought before kings and rulers for my name's sake."

Jesus also says he will help his followers to be strong and he will enable us to confess the one true faith. "I will give you a mouth and wisdom." "And it shall turn to you for a testimony."

The Lord also promises his ongoing protection and care. "But there shall not a hair of your head perish." We have the promise that Christ watches over all those sheep that belong to the Good Shepherd. We may experience persecution, arrest and even death, but no one can take away our faith or our salvation. "In your patience possess ye your souls."

Read this famous passage from Matthew, and note how Jesus explains what we have been looking at from Luke.

Matthew 10:24-32

[24]The disciple is not above his master, nor the servant above his lord.

[25]It is enough for the disciple that he be as his master, and the servant as his lord. If they have called the master of the house Beelzebub, how much more shall they call them of his household?

[26]Fear them not therefore, for there is nothing covered, that shall not be revealed, and hid, that shall not be known.

[27]What I tell you in darkness, that speak ye in light. And what ye hear in the ear, that preach ye upon the housetops.

²⁸Fear not them that kill the body, but are not able to kill the soul. But rather fear him that is able to destroy both soul and body in hell.

²⁹Are not two sparrows sold for a farthing? And one of them shall not fall on the ground without your Father.

³⁰But the very hairs of your head are all numbered.

³¹Fear ye not therefore, ye are of more value than many sparrows.

³²Whosoever therefore shall confess me before men, him will I confess also before my Father which is in heaven.

HOW TO READ THE BIBLE

The Bible is a collection of historical narratives, letters, poetry, prophetic oracles and wisdom literature. It was written over a long period, from about 1500 B.C. to 75 A.D. The Bible is more like a library than just a single book. It contains many different types of literary styles and each book has a specific message and purpose. The Holy Spirit inspired the writers of the Bible, and they wrote exactly what God wanted them to record. Because the Scriptures are inspired, they have a consistent unity from beginning to end.

The Bible tells a single story, a unified narrative that reaches back to the creation of the universe and the beginnings of humanity. It describes how we rebelled against our Creator and how this rebellion ruined perfection. It also describes God's plan of salvation to rescue his fallen creation. The Father will call a specific people to be his servants. From these people, comes Jesus of Nazareth, the promised Messiah of Israel.

The Bible also reveals how this present world will come to an end. God is in control of everything that happens, and all things are working towards the final consummation of God's original design. Our ultimate goal is living eternally in a restored universe that is set free from sin and death. "He will wipe every tear from their eyes. There will be no more death, mourning, crying, or pain, for the old order of things has passed away. Behold! I am making all things new!"

The best way to read the Bible is to read big and read often. Seek to read each book of the Bible, one-by-one. Read God's Word every day and you will soon develop the habit of daily devotionals. Keep a pad and pen handy to jot down questions and insights you may have. Open and close with prayer. Make time each day for these devotionals.

There are many excellent introductions to the Holy Scriptures, commentaries and self-study Bibles available. These can be a great resource to learn the historical background of each book and to understand the teaching and theology of each book. (Be sure and get books written by Bible-believing, Christ-confessing scholars.)

The story of the Bible is not just words written on the page of a book. It is the story of your life and your eternal destiny. The Bible was written so that you might fully enter into this narrative and experience for yourself God's amazing grace in Christ. The Lord calls to us through his Word and we respond with our faith. We trust in his promises. We respond with our worship, prayers and obedience. God himself is calling for you to engage with his Word.

The story of the Bible begins with creation. God not only creates this universe and this planet, but he also makes all plant, animal and marine life. He creates the land, seas, sky and stars. All of this is done according to a specific design and purpose. God's incredible power is on display as he speaks and creation comes into existence. God creates through his Word. "God said, 'Let there be light,' and there was light."

Most especially, God creates humanity in his image. Adam and Eve were created by God to be caretakers of his creation. This earth was designed to be our home and our Creator provided everything we needed for a complete and perfect life. We received a specific vocation: To be good stewards of all that God created.

The Triune God dwelt directly with Adam and Eve in the Garden of Eden and they experienced his direct presence and blessing. They had a perfect knowledge of God and an unbroken relationship of love and trust. At the end of the sixth day of creation, we hear, "And God saw all that he had made and it was very good." That indicates that everything was exactly as God intended it to be. Everything, including humanity, was perfect, complete and holy.

However, we then read that Adam and Eve rebelled against their Creator. They gave in to the devil's temptation to be like God. They decided to go their own way and seek their own wisdom. They wanted to live without God and they rejected his Word. They failed in their calling as stewards. At this point, the Bible becomes a story of good versus evil.

Our rebellion broke the perfection of God's original creation. It introduced sin, death and evil into this world. It broke the perfect communion we had with our loving God. Adam and Eve were driven from the Garden of Eden. Tragedy soon struck in the story of Cain and Abel. Further confusion and rebellion ensued, quickly escalating with the chaos that preceded the flood of Noah. It appeared that evil had overwhelmed humanity. However, there was a fresh start with the family of Noah.

We were originally created for healthy, life-giving relationships: Relationships with God, with each other, with all of creation. Now, we must live with the fracturing of all these relationships. We deal with brokenness, pain, suffering, sickness, heartache, conflict, evil, bloodshed and death. We see the results of the fall all around us every day. We experience it in our own life. The descendants of Noah would continue their sinful ways. The problem of evil remained, even after the flood.

Another result of our rebellion is that we lost the true knowledge of God and the experience of his direct presence. After the fall, the offspring of Adam and Eve will try to find their way back to the source of life, back to the Creator. They will devise any number of philosophies and religions, each trying to make sense of this fallen world. The memory of a lost perfection is deeply engrained in us. We long to be restored to that perfection we have lost. We long to go home. However, by ourselves, we cannot find our way back to God.

The good news is that the Creator reaches out to us through his Word. God comes to us in his mercy and he reveals his plan of salvation for a fallen creation. This plan will center on a specific people that God calls to be his servants. They will be the stewards of his promises. We see the direction of this redemptive plan when God calls Abraham, promising to make him into a great nation. God chooses his family and his descendants, but the ultimate goal is to bless all the peoples on earth and to remove sin and death from this universe.

When Abraham's descendants are enslaved in Egypt, a central pattern is set: God hears their cries for help and he comes to set them free. Moses will lead the people of Israel out of Egypt. This Exodus is the great salvation event of the Old Testament, foreshadowing the greater redemption Christ will accomplish through his death and resurrection.

God makes a covenant with his redeemed nation of Israel at Mount Sinai. The people were to be a light to the nations, showing the world what it means to follow God's ways and Word. They were to be stewards of God's Word and promises.

The Lord promises to bless his people in the new land he is giving them. He will dwell with them in the tabernacle (and temple), he will be their God, and they will be his people. God also warns them that if they are not faithful to his covenant, he will send them away, just as he did with Adam and Eve. In spite of God's repeated warnings through his prophets, Israel seems determined to break the covenant. Therefore, God abandons his holy temple, a sign that his presence will no longer be with his people, and Jerusalem is destroyed by the Babylonians.

Abraham's descendants repeat the failure of Adam and Eve. However, there is still hope. A faithful remnant persevered in Israel. These were the core of believers who continued to follow God's Word. They held on to God's promises. They cried out for help and God came to the rescue.

God's chief promise centered upon a Savior, someone who would crush the head of the serpent. Already back in the Garden of Eden, God gave this promise to Eve. One of her offspring would crush the head of the devil and undo all the damage he caused. This promised offspring of the woman would be the Messiah.

This promise of the Messiah would continue down through the line of Abel, Seth and Noah. Then, it would follow Shem, Abraham, Isaac and Jacob. From Jacob, the promise is narrowed down to the tribe of Judah and then the family of David. The Messiah would come from those faithful believers who continued to trust in God's specific promises. He would be a King and a Savior. "Salvation is from the Jews."

The prophets give us key promises concerning the Messiah and his saving work. The Psalms describe how the Son of David would suffer for our salvation. The stories of the Exodus and the Passover Lamb foreshadow our deliverance. The priesthood and sacrifices point towards the saving work of our Kinsman-Redeemer. The Old Testament gives over 100 specific prophecies about the Messiah, and the Book of Isaiah alone gives over 35 promises about the Savior.

The saving works of our Lord are promised many times in the Old Testament, and those prophecies describe his birth, life, miracles, teaching, betrayal, rejection, suffering, death, burial, resurrection and ascension into heaven. Jesus Christ is the complete fulfillment of Israel's story and a new start for the entire human race. Our Lord recapitulates the story of the Hebrews and brings it to completion. "Out of Egypt, I called my Son."

Death comes through the first man, Adam. However, the resurrection of the dead comes through the Second Adam, Jesus. God's original intention and design is reclaimed in Jesus Christ. He perfectly obeys God's will, despite being repeatedly tempted by the devil. He succeeds where Adam and Eve failed. He defeats the power of evil. He perfectly obeyed God's Law and then gave up his perfect life as the great atoning sacrifice for the sins of the world.

The Christ completes and fulfills all of the Old Testament requirements that foreshadowed his saving work. These include the Sabbath, circumcision, the food laws, the festivals, the priesthood and sacrifices, the temple and land. All of these practices and institutions foreshadowed our Lord's ministry. Therefore, he has brought them to completion. "These are a shadow of the things to come: The reality, however, is found in Christ."

The resurrection of our Lord is the great sign that the new creation has begun. The resurrection of Israel's King shows that the great enemies of God's creation – sin and death and evil – have been totally defeated. In Christ, we have reconciliation with our Creator and the image of God is now being restored within us by the work of the Holy Spirit. "Therefore, if anyone is in Christ, he is a new creation; the old has gone, the new has come!"

We see the intentions of God revealed in the ministry and work of Jesus healing the sick and casting out demons. He comes to reclaim and restore God's broken creation. Our Lord heals the sick and forgives sinners. He comes to make us whole and complete. He overcomes the powers of evil and he defeats the devil. All of this happens through his saving work that culminates on the cross and in the empty tomb.

The Messiah is the Son of God in human flesh. "The Word became flesh and dwelt among us, full of grace and truth." The incarnation is the great turning point of all history. This is the fulfillment of all of the promises made to the people of God in the Old Testament. Jesus is the Word of God made flesh. He comes to teach us about the Father and to show us the way back home. Jesus Christ brings us back to our Maker and he pays the price for our rebellion. In him, we are restored and forgiven.

"All this is from God, who reconciled us to himself in Christ and gave us the ministry of reconciliation: That God was reconciling the world to himself in Christ, not counting men's sins against them."

This promised restoration is yours today, by faith. On the last day, you will enter into it fully and completely. The story of the Bible moves on towards that grand finale. Something great awaits us! This promise of what is yet to come helps us to deal with the present. This hope of the coming new creation lifts up our hearts. We know that better days are coming soon.

Now, in this earthly life, we are called to be good stewards of what God has entrusted to us. However, like Israel, we are often prone to rebellion. We resist God's will, too. We also need to repent and confess our brokenness. On this side of heaven, we will never be perfect. Therefore, we pray every day, "Forgive us our trespasses." We seek to grow stronger in our faith. We strive to follow God's way and wisdom. We reject what is evil and pursue what is good. "Put on the new self, created to be like God in true righteousness and holiness."

Here, the letters of the New Testament can help us to grow in our faith and obedience to God's Word. The four Gospels describe the first Advent of our Lord. They extensively describe the work and teachings of Christ. The Book of Acts shows us how the message of the Messiah's resurrection victory changed the lives of all different types of people. This message of the Gospel is for all people, Jew and Gentile – everyone – regardless of race, culture or nationality. This universal message goes forth even to this day, all around the world.

Your calling now is to hear this message of God's reconciliation in Christ and apply it to your heart and soul. Each day, confess your sins and receive absolution. Each day, seek to become more Christ-like as the Holy Spirit leads you in sanctification. Strive to be a witness to the Risen Lord. Share the gift you have received. Testify to God's mercy and grace. Dedicate your life to Christ by living a life of faith, humility and love. Be a servant to others and a good steward of what God has entrusted to you.

Finally, as you read the Bible, watch for two distinct messages: Law and Gospel. You need to properly distinguish between these two messages and not mix them together. Both Law and Gospel are the Word of God. Both can be found in the Old and New Testaments. (It is not the case that the Old Testament is only Law, and the New Testament is only the Gospel. The Old contains Gospel, and the New Testament has the Law, too.)

The Law tells us what to do and not to do. These are God's moral commandments, which are given to all of humanity, and they are not subject to change. This Law is meant to give order and structure to our life. In effect, God says, "I created you, and this is how I want you to live and act." The Ten Commandments are the great summation of the Law.

Jesus summarizes the Law this way: "Love the Lord your God with all your heart and with all your soul and with all your mind. This is the first and greatest commandment. And the second is like it: Love your neighbor as yourself. All the Law and the Prophets hang on these two commandments."

The problem here is that we cannot keep the Law because we are sinners. That is why when you read something in the Bible that disturbs you, that is the Law accusing you. The Law shows us our sins. It is like a mirror that reveals our true state when we stand before God. Law speaks a message of accusation and judgment. It declares that we are lost sinners who deserve to be punished. It tells us that we have not loved God the way we should. We have not loved our neighbor.

The Gospel, on the other hand, tells us about what God has done to save lost sinners. "God so loved the world that he gave his Son." The Gospel is good news: It describes God's gift of grace in Jesus Christ. God gave his Son to suffer that punishment we deserve. The Gospel is God's promise of forgiveness, life and salvation. It shows us our Savior. It declares that God loves you and your sins are forgiven. You are now a child of God!

The Gospel also empowers us to do good works and to obey God's commands. This is the free and spontaneous obedience of the believer. It is our response to God's gift of grace. These good works are the fruits that the Holy Spirit produces in us. It is God working in our lives and God empowering us to obey his Word. This is possible only because we are connected to Jesus Christ, the Messiah of Israel.

Jesus says, "I am the vine; you are the branches. If you remain in me, you will bear much fruit; apart from me, you can do nothing. This is to my Father's glory, that you bear much fruit, showing yourselves to be my disciples. As the Father has loved me, so have I loved you. Now remain in my love. If you obey my commands, you will remain in my love, just as I have obeyed my Father's commands and remain in his love."

We remain in God's love through the power of his Messiah and the promised Holy Spirit. We remain connected to the Vine as we experience his wondrous love each day. By God's grace, we can bear much fruit, to the glory of our heavenly Father. May God the Holy Spirit enlighten you as you read the Word of God!

Our Lord promises, "When the Counselor comes, whom I will send to you from the Father, the Spirit of truth who goes out from the Father, he will testify about me. And you also must testify, for you have been with me from the beginning." Amen!

ABOUT THE AUTHOR:

Volker Heide has served as a pastor in the
Lutheran Church – Missouri Synod for 30
years. He attended Concordia Seminary in St.
Louis, Missouri (M. Div., New Testament
Theology), and also the United States
Merchant Marine Academy in Kings Point,
New York (B.S., Nautical Science). This is his
second book.

Made in the USA
Middletown, DE
05 September 2020